Access to History

General Editor: Keith Randell

From Bismarck to Hitler: Germany 1890-1933

Geoff Layton

Hodder & Stoughton

A MEMBER OF THE HODDER HEADLINE GROUP

The cover illustration is a portrait of Hindenburg by Hugo Vogel (courtesy of Bildarchiv Preussischer Kulturbesitz).

Some other titles in the series:

France: The Third Republic 1870-1914   ISBN 0 340 55569 6
Keith Randell

The Unification of Germany 1815-90   ISBN 0 340 51810 3
Andrina Stiles

Germany: The Third Reich 1933-45   ISBN 0 340 53846 3
Geoff Layton

Italy: Liberalism and Fascism 1870-1945   ISBN 0 340 54548 8
Mark Robson

Reaction and Revolutions: Russia 1881-1924   ISBN 0 340 53336 6
Michael Lynch

Rivalry and Accord: International Relations 1870-1914   ISBN 0 340 51806 5
John Lowe

Orders: please contact Bookpoint Ltd, 130 Milton Park, Abingdon, Oxon OX14 4SB. Telephone: (44) 01235 400414, Fax: (44) 01235 400454. Lines are open from 9.00-6.00, Monday to Saturday, with a 24 hour message answering service. Email address: orders@bookpoint.co.uk

British Library Cataloguing in Publication Data

Layton, Geoff
    From Bismarck to Hitler: Germany
    1890-1933.-(Access to History Series)
    I. Title   II. Series
    943.08

ISBN 0-340-59488-8

First published 1995
Impression number   12   11   10   9
Year   2004   2003   2002   2001

Typeset by Sempringham Publishing Services, Bedford.
Printed in Great Britain for Hodder & Stoughton Educational, a division of Hodder Headline Plc, 338 Euston Road, London NW1 3BH by The Bath Press, Bath

Contents

Preface

To the general reader

Although the *Access to History* series has been designed with the needs of students studying the subject at higher examination levels very much in mind, it also has a great deal to offer the general reader. The main body of the text (i.e. ignoring the Study Guides at the ends of chapters) forms a readable and yet stimulating survey of a coherent topic as studied by historians. However, each author's aim has not merely been to provide a clear explanation of what happened in the past (to interest and inform): it has also been assumed that most readers wish to be stimulated into thinking further about the topic and to form opinions of their own about the significance of the events that are described and discussed (to be challenged). Thus, although no prior knowledge of the topic is expected on the reader's part, she or he is treated as an intelligent and thinking person throughout. The author tends to share ideas and possibilities with the reader, rather than passing on numbers of so-called 'historical truths'.

To the student reader

There are many ways in which the series can be used by students studying History at a higher level. It will, therefore, be worthwhile thinking about your own study strategy before you start your work on this book. Obviously, your strategy will vary depending on the aim you have in mind, and the time for study that is available to you.

If, for example, you want to acquire a general overview of the topic in the shortest possible time, the following approach will probably be the most effective:

1 Read Chapter 1 and think about its contents.
2 Read the 'Making notes' section at the end of Chapter 2 and decide whether it is necessary for you to read this chapter.
3 If it is, read the chapter, stopping at each heading to note down the main points that have been made.
4 Repeat stage 2 (and stage 3 where appropriate) for all the other chapters.

If, however, your aim is to gain a thorough grasp of the topic, taking however much time is necessary to do so, you may benefit from carrying out the same procedure with each chapter, as follows:

1 Read the chapter as fast as you can, and preferably at one sitting.
2 Study the flow diagram at the end of the chapter, ensuring that you understand the general 'shape' of what you have just read.

3 Read the 'Making notes' section (and the 'Answering essay questions' section, if there is one) and decide what further work you need to do on the chapter. In particularly important sections of the book, this will involve reading the chapter a second time and stopping at each heading to think about (and to write a summary of) what you have just read.

4 Attempt the 'Source-based questions' section. It will sometimes be sufficient to think through your answers, but additional understanding will often be gained by forcing yourself to write them down.

When you have finished the main chapters of the book, study the 'Further Reading' section and decide what additional reading (if any) you will do on the topic.

This book has been designed to help make your studies both enjoyable and successful. If you can think of ways in which this could have been done more effectively, please write to tell me. In the meantime, I hope that you will gain greatly from your study of History.

Keith Randell

Acknowledgements

The Publishers would like to thank the following for permission to reproduce illustrations in this volume:

Cover - Hindenburg, Bildarchiv Preussischer Kulturbesitz
Ullstein Bilderdiens, Berlin p. 17; AKG, London (from *Simplicissimus* Vol XIII p. 666, 28 December 1908) p. 37; Weimar Archive, Telford p. 61, p. 78, p. 101; Karl Arnold / Wiener Library, London p. 127; Pictorial Nostalgia p. 101.

Every effort has been made to trace and acknowledge ownership of copyright. The Publishers will be glad to make suitable arrangements with any copyright holders whom it has not been possible to contact.

CHAPTER 1

Introduction: From Bismarck to Hitler

Several years after the event the English correspondent of *The Times* described the scenes in Berlin on 30 January 1933, the day of Hitler's appointment as chancellor of Germany:

1 Berlin was buzzing like a beehive from morning till night, the nerves of four million people were quivering like harp strings ... The Brownshirts were hilariously jubilant. The last trench had been taken, the brown armies had the freedom of the streets ... I
5 stood at a window of the Foreign Office that night and watched them tramping endlessly past, while their bands played 'Fridericus Rex' and the 'Horst Wessel' march. Hour after hour they poured with their torchlights through the once forbidden Brandenburger Tor ... marching with the triumphant ecstatic air of soldiers taking
10 possession of a long beleaguered city. Opposite me were two palaces, one a grey ponderous building in the Wilhelmian style of architecture, the other a clean-cut four-square building, a typical product of the Germany of 1918-33. Behind a lighted window of the old building stood a massive old man [President Hindenburg].
15 I saw him nod his head continually as the bands blared and the Brownshirts marched past, throwing their heads back and their eyes right to salute him. But they were not there to honour him. His day was done. The salute to the old man was perfunctory. Fifty yards down the street in the new palace was another window, on a
20 higher level, open, with the spotlights playing on it, a young man leaning out ... A colleague found beauty in the scene. "Hitler looks marvellous", he said. The old and the new. Field Marshall and Bohemian Corporal. Hitler and Hindenburg. Tramp, tramp, tramp, blare, blare, blare. Hour after hour they came.

Although this book focuses on the history of Germany from 1890 to 1933, it is almost impossible for the historian and the student to escape the implications of the fateful day which brought the period to its close and ushered in the Third Reich. History unfortunately is unable to provide alternative endings and the historian has no choice but to interpret the past with the perspective provided. And so, over half a century later, the Nazi dictatorship still casts its baleful shadow across the history of modern Germany. The desire to understand and explain Nazism is at the heart of many of the debates of modern German history, though as will be seen, it has not, and indeed should not, be the sole purpose behind a study of Imperial and Weimar Germany.

1 The Historical Issues

In his influential book *The Course of German History*, first published in 1945, Britain's most renowned twentieth century historian A.J.P. Taylor wrote: 'It was no more a mistake for the German people to end up with Hitler than it is an accident when a river flows into the sea'. The central thrust of Taylor's interpretation was that the dynamic unleashed by the process of unification in the nineteenth century gave way to the imperial ambitions of Wilhelm II and logically culminated in the tyranny of Hitler's Third Reich. His view that the Third Reich was a natural outgrowth of German history proved to be generally very popular in Britain, partly because it was expressed in his easy-going literary style, and partly because it struck a ready chord with the generation whose lives were clouded by the events of 1914 to 1945. However, in the immediate post-war era there was little sympathy for such a direct link amongst Germany's leading historians who had been educated in the conservative-nationalist tradition of German historiography. They viewed history as the result of the 'primacy of foreign policy' and the key issues were war, diplomacy and high politics, which were decided by a few 'great men'. In this way the tendency was to interpret Hitler and Nazism in rather apologetic terms as an aberration totally at odds with Germany's historical development under the *Kaiserreich* and the Weimar Republic.

Since that time there has been a veritable 'revolution' in German historical studies. The easy calm was shattered by the publication in 1961 of Fritz Fischer's *Griff nach der Weltmacht* (Germany's Aims in the First World War), which advanced the thesis that Germany's objectives in July 1914 had indeed been offensive and had been intended to establish German hegemony over continental Europe. The significance of this was profound indeed, for not only did it suggest a similarity between the foreign policy aims of Imperial Germany in 1914 and Nazi Germany in 1939, but it also implied that there was a clear line of continuity between the two regimes. Such views stimulated the development of what have become known as 'structuralist' interpretations, which sought to explain history through a detailed examination and synthesis of social, political and economic forces - what became known as the 'primacy of domestic politics'. Foremost amongst the exponents of this methodology is H.U. Wehler, whose book, *Das Deutsche Kaiserreich 1871-1918*, published in 1973, continues to be regarded as a vital text on the period. The emergence of the 'structuralist' history (sometimes also referred to as 'critical social history') in the 1960s and 1970s was unashamedly motivated by a desire to understand and explain the establishment of the Third Reich. To that end it not only emphasised the vital importance of continuity in German history from 1871 to 1945, but it also upheld the idea of a German *Sonderweg* or 'special path of development' which propounded that

Germany's process of modernisation had somehow diverged from other countries and was somehow 'peculiar'.

Structuralist interpretations exerted an enormous influence on our understanding of modern German history and in many respects they came to be viewed as the 'new orthodoxy'. However, since the early 1980s structuralism has been forced to contend with an increasingly influential revisionist tendency which has generally been led by British and American historians. For example, the Anglo-German historian Röhl, who has produced the most important recent study of the Kaiser and Imperial Germany (*The Kaiser and His Court*), re-focused attention on the individuals, the personalities (as opposed to the structural elites) at the very heart of government. On the other hand, Blackbourn and Eley in their book *The Peculiarities of German History* have concentrated their research and analysis away from the political centre in an attempt to write what has been deemed 'history from below'. In this way such historians have come to question some of the assumptions about structuralist history. In particular, what were the exact natures of the continuities in German history? And how valid is the concept of the German *Sonderweg* as an explanation of modern German history?

However, although these broad issues of Germany's historical development have a very important role to play in the search for understanding, they do create a number of further problems. First, they inevitably bring the emotive and highly charged moral overtones of the Nazi era into the picture. And secondly, they can all too easily give the impression that the years 1890-1933 were simply a kind of prologue to the main event. Not only might such an impression tend to reinforce the view that all roads lead to 1933 - a dangerous and loaded assumption in the light of the continuity argument referred to above - it might also have the effect of reducing the significance of 1890-1933 as a period worthy of study in its own right.

This book is therefore conceived with two perspectives very much in mind. Firstly, it is written from the stand-point that there are key historical issues and debates to be considered within the time-frame 1890 to 1933. Who really did control Imperial Germany? How responsible was Germany for the outbreak of the First World War? How and why did the First World War have such a dramatic effect on Germany? And did the Weimar Republic ever really stand any chance of long-term survival? These are some of the crucial questions considered in Chapters 2 to 7, which form the core of the book. Secondly, it is written from the stand-point that the period 1890-1933 must be examined within the broader context of German history, and particularly of the years 1871-1945. To this end, the next section examines the Bismarckian legacy, whilst the broader issues of continuity in German history and the German *Sonderweg*, though occasionally alluded to, are discussed in detail in Chapter 8.

2 The Bismarckian Legacy

Wilhelm I, King of Prussia (1861-88) and Emperor of Germany (1871-88), once drily remarked about his relationship with Bismarck: 'It isn't easy to be an emperor under a chancellor like this one'. However, despite the heartache and frustration implied by this comment, Bismarck and his sovereign worked together most effectively for just over a quarter of a century. Such an understanding did not prove possible with the accession in June 1888 of the Emperor's grandson, Wilhelm II (1888-1918). In less than two years the two men had fallen out on both a personal and a political level, and on 18 March 1890 Bismarck proffered his resignation. Wilhelm II gladly accepted it.

Few contemporaries in Germany lamented Bismarck's fall from favour. Although the 'Iron Chancellor' had successfully forged the unification of Germany out of a collection of autonomous states and had then managed the new nation's affairs for nearly twenty years, by which time the Second Empire had developed into the most powerful state on mainland Europe, there were many who believed that Bismarck had outlived his usefulness and that the young Kaiser offered a viable new course which was preferable. From the outset then, the legacy bequeathed by Bismarck was viewed as a mixed blessing.

The constitution of the German Empire drawn up by Bismarck in 1871 was a most curious contrivance. It has been said that it 'did not fit easily into any category known to the political scientists', and that in essence it was an 'uneasy compromise between the forces of conservative federalism, the liberal unitary principle and the military might of Prussia'. Bismarck's attempt to reconcile such a diverse mixture of guiding principles within a structure of quite considerable complexity created difficulties which were not initially apparent but which gradually emerged with the passing of time.

The Reich in fact consisted of 25 sovereign states - four kingdoms, six grand duchies, four duchies, eight principalities and three free cities, plus the imperial territory of Alsace-Lorraine annexed in 1871 - which had theoretically come together voluntarily and enjoyed equality of status. However, in reality there was no disguising the dominant role of Prussia. Prussia consisted of two-thirds of the Reich territory and, as King of Prussia, Wilhelm II was automatically Emperor of Germany. In this capacity he enjoyed great authority as of right: he had the final word over the direction of Germany's foreign policy; he was commander-in-chief of all armed forces within the empire both in peace and war; and he alone could appoint and dismiss the executive - the chancellor and the state secretaries who made up the imperial government. Such were the substantial powers available to Wilhelm II, if he had the will to exert them.

Bismarck's concession to federalism was institutionalised in the *Bundesrat* (Federal Council). It consisted of 58 representatives from the

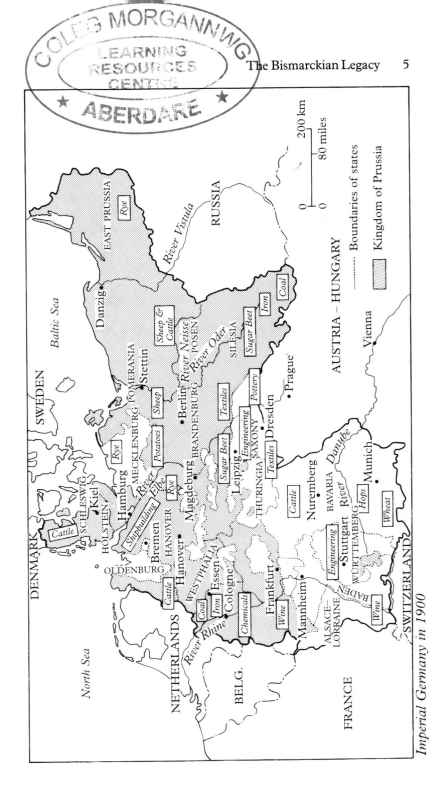

Imperial Germany in 1900

various state governments and was theoretically the most important decision-making body in the empire. It alone had the right to make changes to the constitution and its agreement was required for all legislation. Yet the influence of Prussia was paramount, since it was entitled to 17 of the seats at the council table and as any military or constitutional issue could be vetoed by the opposition of just 14 votes, Prussia was able to guarantee its privileged position within the political structure of the empire.

However, it is all too easy to underestimate the powers of the various states individually. Although the imperial government had complete control over foreign policy and defence, trade and tariffs, and currency and banking, responsibility for education, justice and health was devolved to the states. Most significantly, only the states could raise direct taxes. The imperial government was prohibited from levying a national income tax and was therefore dependent upon indirect taxes such as customs duties and sales taxes. This was a factor of great importance, since it acted as a major constraint on the expenditure of the imperial government.

The third major element in Bismarck's constitutional framework was the *Reichstag* (Imperial Parliament), which was directly elected by universal suffrage and secret ballot. However, this apparent concession to liberal democracy was in reality limited in scope. For although Bismarck had always desired the co-operation of the *Reichstag* in the passage of legislation - and he went to considerable lengths to secure pro-government majorities - it did not enjoy the same privileges and status as did the British House of Commons at the end of the nineteenth century. It was not permitted to introduce legislation, but could only discuss and ratify those proposals forwarded by the *Bundesrat* and the imperial government. Above all, the imperial government was not accountable to it. The *Reichstag* was therefore a representative assembly without real power - which, of course, was as Bismarck intended.

The implications of this constitutional structure for a Germany without Bismarck were a cause for concern. The *Kaiserreich* bore the stamp both of its creator and the circumstances of its creation. Above all, it had aimed to institutionalise the position and power of Bismarck himself and to preserve the privileges of Prussia and its ruling class by a complex system of checks and balances. Yet, even with Bismarck still at the helm there were occasions when political deadlock had resulted in a worrying inertia. It was already clear that the power structure was incoherent. From 1888 this situation had been exacerbated by the accession of an emperor who was no longer prepared to sit on the sidelines. Only then did the weakness of the chancellor's position reveal itself. The chancellor was solely responsible to the emperor and as Wilhelm II wished to exert a more personal rule than his grandfather, this was bound to lead to confusion in the executive unless both emperor and chancellor showed a mutual respect and shared a common political outlook. In 1890 such problems would not have been insurmountable if only the political system had exhibited a degree of flexibility. However, the entrenched rigidity of Bismarck's constitutional structure proved to be a major weakness. There was only very limited scope for adaptation to changing circumstances. And circumstances were changing fundamentally. Germany in the second half of the nineteenth century was in the midst of a radical and rapid social and economic transformation. It had experienced a fast industrial 'take-off' in the 1850s and 1860s, and, despite a down-turn in the trade cycle after 1873, there is no doubt that by 1890 two major landmarks had been achieved: Germany had crossed the line dividing an agrarian from an industrial state; and it had surpassed all its economic rivals on the continent of Europe, though it had not yet overtaken Great Britain. The social ramifications of these startling economic changes were enormous. Not only were the traditional social structures altered, but literally millions of ordinary people had to come to terms with dramatic changes in their lifestyle - which in turn affected traditional codes of behaviour and ties of loyalty and allegiance.

Such was the nature of the Bismarckian legacy in 1890, when the young Wilhelm II decided to assume the 'personal rule' of his empire.

Studying 'From Bismarck to Hitler'

This introductory chapter should have enabled you to identify the main historical issues and debates raised by this period of history and also to familiarise yourself with the historical background.

If you have already studied nineteenth century German history, the second section of the chapter should present no problems at all. Indeed, it would probably be better to look back on your previous notes and then only jot down anything which seems particularly unfamiliar to you. However, if modern German history is a new historical topic for you, then you will have to read this section very carefully and try to understand as much as you can. Alternatively, you could look at the companion volume in this series, *The Unification of Germany, 1815-90.*

The first section is quite demanding and many students will probably find some of the ideas difficult to grasp. Don't worry. It is simply intended to highlight some of the key issues. If at this stage you can simply aim to keep some of these in mind as you work on the rest of the book, it will help you when we come to our concluding chapter. If you can write brief answers to the following questions, you should have identified and understood the most important points:

1. In what ways does later German history affect our perspective on the years 1890-1933?

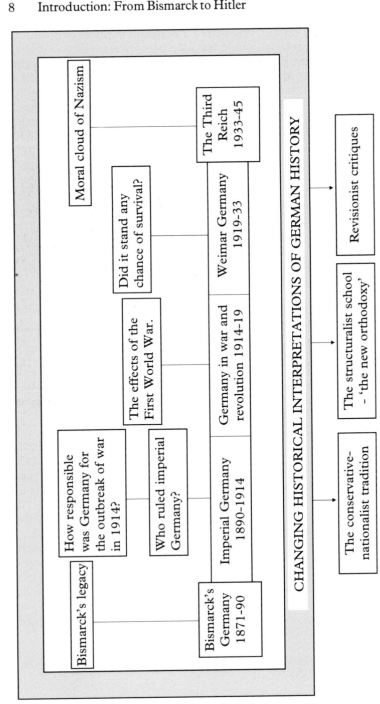

CHANGING HISTORICAL INTERPRETATIONS OF GERMAN HISTORY

Bismarck's legacy

How responsible was Germany for the outbreak of war in 1914?

Who ruled imperial Germany?

The effects of the First World War.

Did it stand any chance of survival?

Moral cloud of Nazism

Bismarck's Germany 1871-90

Imperial Germany 1890-1914

Germany in war and revolution 1914-19

Weimar Germany 1919-33

The Third Reich 1933-45

The conservative-nationalist tradition

The structuralist school – 'the new orthodoxy'

Revisionist critiques

Summary – Introduction: From Bismarck to Hitler

2. What is meant by a) 'continuity' in German history?
                     b) 'the German *Sonderweg*'?
3. What are the implications of these two terms for historians studying modern German history?

When you have done this you will then be in a position to study and think about some of the more specific issues of historical significance in the body of the text:

i)   The structure and governance of Imperial Germany - Chapters 2-3.
ii) German responsibility for the outbreak of the First World War - Chapter 3 (this must also be related directly to your study of international relations and the origins of the First World War).
iii) The vital impact of the First World War on Germany - Chapter 4.
iv) The Weimar Republic's search for stability - Chapters 5-6 (this will not only be closely related to your study of the Peace Settlement of 1919-20, but it will also be vital if you want to compare post-war developments across Europe).
v)   The collapse of Weimar - Chapter 7 (this should also closely complement your study of National Socialism and the Third Reich).

Because German history is so central to the history of later modern Europe, all these themes are frequently used as the focus for examination questions. In addition, you will also see from the above that the period needs to be studied in conjunction with several other main-stream topics. If all this suggests that a lot of work is involved, it should also imply that your efforts are likely to be well-rewarded in the end.

CHAPTER 2

The Structure of Wilhelmine Germany, 1890-1914

At the height of the diplomatic crisis in July 1914 which eventually culminated in the First World War the Austrian foreign minister asked in frustration: 'Who actually rules in Berlin?'. It was a pertinent question, though not only in the short-term context, for it neatly encapsulates the key issues facing historians of the *Kaiserreich* to this day. What exactly was the power structure within Imperial Germany? Who exerted the decisive influence on policy and events? What were the objectives of that leadership? In order to address these issues this chapter attempts to examine the major forces - personal and impersonal - in the political, social and economic life of the *Kaiserreich*. The next chapter will then consider the development of Germany's domestic and foreign policies in these years. It may then be possible to draw some tentative conclusions to the above questions about Wilhelmine Germany.

1 Economic and Social Change

a) The Economy

Wilhelm II came to the throne of a state whose economy had already successfully completed in the early 1870s what economic historians call the 'take-off' into sustained economic growth. By 1890 further economic development had led to the predominance of the industrial sector over its agricultural counterpart. And yet, despite the occasional down-turn in the trade cycle, for example in 1891 and 1901, the years 1890 to 1914 were to witness another period of sustained economic expansion with rates of growth reaching seven or eight per cent per annum. Such phenomenal figures were brought about partly by the continued increases in production in those industries associated with the first phase of industrialization - coal, iron, heavy engineering and textiles - but also by the diversification of the economy into more sophisticated areas of manufacture - steel, chemicals and electrics (see the table on pages 11-12).

By 1914 Germany had become Europe's industrial superpower. It had nearly caught up with Britain's level of coal production and it had already exceeded Britain's level of iron production. It was by far the largest manufacturer of cotton cloth on the continent. However, what really marked out the German economy in the 25 years before the First World War was the expansion of the newer industries. German steel production increased nearly nine-fold in this period - by 1914 German output was double that of Britain. Even more impressive was the emergence of the electrical, chemical and motor construction industries.

Two German firms, AEG and Siemens (whose founder had developed the dynamo) came to dominate the world market, so that by 1913 it is reckoned that nearly 50 per cent of the world's electrical products originated from Germany. It was a similar story in the chemicals industry, where the extraction of potash and potassium salts massively increased the availability of fertilizers, and where research and development in the light (fine) sector of chemicals manufacture gave Germany a world lead in the preparation of dyes and pharmaceutical products.

The Development of the German Economy

1 Population (in millions)

Year	Total	Per Cent in Towns over 2,000
1871	41.1	36.1
1880	42.2	41.4
1890	49.4	42.5
1900	56.4	54.4
1910	64.9	60.0

2 Output of Heavy Industry (in millions of tons)

(a) Coal

Year	Germany	UK
1871	37.7	119.2
1880	59.1	149.3
1890	89.2	184.5
1900	149.5	228.8
1910	222.2	268.7

(b) Steel

Year	Germany	UK
1871	0.14	0.41
1880	0.69	1.32
1890	2.13	3.64
1900	6.46	4.98
1910	13.10	6.48

3 Index of Industrial Production (1913 = 100)

Year	
1871	21.0
1880	49.4
1890	57.3
1900	61.0
1910	86.0
1913	100.0

4   Balance of Payments (in millions of marks)

Year	Imports	Exports	Visible Balance	Invisible Balance	Overall Balance
1880	2,814	2,923	+ 109	+ 168	+ 277
1890	4,162	3,335	- 827	+ 1,249	+ 422
1900	5,769	4,611	- 1,158	+ 1,566	+ 408
1910	8,927	7,475	- 1,452	+ 2,211	+ 759

5   Structure of Labour Force (in millions of workers)

Sector	1875	1895	1913
Agriculture	9.23	9.79	10.7
Mining	0.29	0.43	0.86
Industry	5.15	7.52	10.86
Transport	0.35	0.62	1.17
Commerce/Banking	1.12	1.97	3.47
Hotels/Domestic	1.49	1.57	1.54
Defence	0.43	0.61	0.86
Other	0.59	0.89	1.49
Total	18.64	23.40	30.97

The economic picture these figures present seems clear-cut. Germany had rapidly built on its earlier foundations and by 1914 had grown into the most powerful industrial economy on the European continent, with a share of world trade which rivalled that of Britain and its empire. How and why did this come about?

Firstly, Germany's population continued to grow rapidly - there were one-third more Germans in 1910 than there had been in 1890. This provided both the market and the labour force for an expanding economy. Moreover, the balance of the population was towards the younger generations and this facilitated mobility and skills adaptation, which were both vital in the change-over to a more advanced level of economic production. The availability and accessibility of raw materials were also a necessity and Germany was generously blessed with natural resources: coal from the Ruhr, Saar and Silesia; iron-ore from Alsace-Lorraine and the Ruhr; potash from Alsace-Lorraine. Thus, the huge demand for energy, iron-steel products and chemicals could be met to a large extent from domestic supplies which was a huge benefit for the balance of payments. Other geographical advantages included navigable rivers, such as the Rhine and the Elbe, and the broad flat northern plain which was so suited to the construction of railways. Such natural advantages were complemented by human skills and proficiency. Germany had probably the best elementary education system in the world. And, perhaps even more importantly, its institutes of higher education not only provided for the traditional scholar, but also made increasing provision for those with technical skills (though it should also be noted that all such establishments remained socially very selective).

Another area of expertise was the German banking system which had traditionally played such an important role in trade and industry. In the last decade of the century the banking system expanded enormously. Free from any kind of state control, German banks pursued an adventurous policy of generous long-term credit facilities. This in turn led the big banks to become directly involved in industrial research and development, as their own representatives were often invited on to the boards of directors of firms - thus cementing a close partnership between the banking and commercial sectors of the economy. The banks were also instrumental in the development of a distinctly German feature of industrialization - the growth of cartels (trusts). In Britain and the USA the idea of a group of businessmen combining together to control prices, production levels and marketing was frowned upon as against the spirit of free enterprise. In Germany they were accepted and legally protected. Indeed, the state even encouraged their development. They were viewed as a sensible means of achieving economies of scale, by removing unnecessary competition and by facilitating development and invest-ment, especially in times of economic recession. By 1905 366 cartels existed according to a government investigation (compared to only 90 in 1885) and whole areas of German industry had been 'cartelised'. To many contemporaries cartels were typical of the efficient large-scale and productive nature of the German industrial economy - though latter-day economic historians have questioned whether they really did benefit the German economy in the long-run.

b) German Society

In simple human terms the impact of this rapid structural transforma-tion into an industrial economy meant that millions of ordinary people were forced to come to terms with fundamental changes in their way of life. Admittedly, some of the more rural districts such as Bavaria and Pomerania remained in a sort of time-warp, but few could escape the consequences of change. The difficulty for the historian is trying to draw some meaningful conclusions about the social effects of these changes without being accused of over-generalizing or of social theorizing. Such difficulties are even more pronounced in the case of German social history, since the traditional sociological analysis on the basis of classes is complicated by the existence of three other lines of division: religious denomination; regional affiliation; and the national identity of minority peoples (especially Poles, Danes, and Alsatians). Bismarck may have unified Germany, but religious, regional and national feelings were still very powerful influences which cut across the various classes of German society. This is perhaps most clearly shown by the solidity of the vote for the Catholic Centre Party (see page 24), especially in Bavaria and the Rhineland, and the success of Catholic trade unions in providing an alternative (albeit a minority one) to the socialist trade unions. It is also surely significant that over ten per cent of the *Reichstag's* seats continued to be won by deputies supporting one of the minority nationalist groupings - amongst which was included the Guelphs who campaigned for an independent Hanover!

Bearing in mind these important qualifying factors, what then were the main social and sociological features of Wilhelmine Germany? Surprisingly, in the light of the fundamental economic changes, German society seems to have remained divided along traditional class lines, and what mobility there was tended to be within a class rather than movement between different classes. Divisions were maintained and it was difficult to achieve higher social status on the grounds of wealth or expertise. Thus, as one historian has written, 'the large majority of working class sons did not leave their class; the majority of the lower middle class continued to come from the lower middle class' (Kaelble). The prejudices of class, religion and race acted as very effective barriers to greater integration - and this was seen in the education system, the professions and the business world, and most prominently at the apex of society, where the higher levels of the civil service and the army remained predominantly the preserve of the nobility.

The landed nobility (*Junkers*) continued to be an extremely powerful force in society, although in economic terms many in this class were beginning to feel the pinch. Agriculture was in relative decline vis-a-vis industry and those landowners who failed to modernize production methods or who did not adapt to changing market conditions were likely to find their financial position under threat. And yet the nobility still regarded its privileged social status within the institutions as not only essential to maintaining the traditions and values of German society, but also as a right and proper reflection of its social superiority built up over many generations.

The most direct threat to the nobility's supremacy came from the wealthy new industrialists. However, most research suggests that successful Wilhelminian businessmen preferred to purchase privileges and to flaunt their wealth in an attempt to emulate the *Junkers* rather than to supersede them. After all, the National Liberals (see page 22) were in the main representatives of business and industry and their policies and actions became increasingly conservative and supportive of the status quo.

The middle ranks of the middle class were also expanding. White collar workers in industry, education and the bureaucracy were in great demand for their scientific, technical or administrative skills. But here too the tendency was to try to keep things as they were rather than to seek change. Teachers and civil servants, for example, were classified as *Beamte* (state officials), and in return for accepting the state's strict regulations of employment they were guaranteed rights of tenure and certain privileges, such as pensions. Such status was highly cherished and widely respected.

However, for the old *Mittelstand* (lower-middle class) of artisans and small-scale traders times were not so good - and the problem went a lot deeper than merely coping with the down-turns in the trade cycle. The *Mittelstand* found itself squeezed between the more powerful economic forces of a unionized working class and the larger, more productive enterprises of big business. As a result, resentment and disenchantment led many in this class to look back on the pre-industrial age as a golden bygone era. It was also to spawn a naive belief that their fears might be overcome by supporting the political solutions of the conservative and authoritarian right.

At the bottom of the social pyramid was the mass of the population who made up the labouring classes - agricultural and industrial. For the smallholders and landless labourers life was particularly difficult. The economic problems of agriculture at this time combined with the growth in population meant that it was difficult to make farming viable. In the south and west of Germany, where smallholding tenancies predominated, families were often forced to divide the land between children who then combined farming with other part-time occupations. In the east, the labourers on the estates of the *Junkers* had little option but to accept the imposed wage cuts. Not surprisingly, to many on the land industrial employment seemed an attractive option - and so the drift to the cities continued.

However, industrial city life presented its own problems. Although employment rates were very good - unemployment only went above three per cent in one year between 1900 and 1914 - and average real wages increased by 25 per cent between 1895 and 1913, living and working conditions remained dismally poor. Thus, for most working people life was divided between long hours in often unhealthy workplaces and the cold cramped accommodation which represented home. As one leading historian has succinctly put it: 'Some 30 per cent of all family households in this prosperous Second Empire lived in destitution and abject misery'.

There is little doubt therefore that the rapid pace of economic change in Wilhelmine Germany had a fundamental effect upon the equilibrium of an already diverse society. Traditional structures and values were still very strong, but economic progress inevitably generated rivalry, tensions and dislocation. It was the problem of balancing the old and the new, of accommodating the various interest groups in Wilhelmine society which the political system somehow had to manage.

2 The Wilhelmine Political System

a) The Emperor and his Court

Whether one should start an analysis of the political system of Wilhelmine Germany with the Kaiser is an issue of historical debate in itself. Many historians would strongly argue that such an approach immediately stamps on German history an excessively 'personalistic' mark, by which they mean it becomes too closely identified with one individual. This is certainly not the intended purpose of starting this section by discussing the emperor and his court. It is simply a recognition that the role of the Kaiser still remains one of several vital issues in the historical debate about the *Kaiserreich*.

Wilhelm II was born in 1859 the eldest child of Crown Prince Friedrich (Kaiser Friedrich III for just 99 days in 1888) and Victoria, the eldest daughter of Queen Victoria. Even his birth has become the focus of historical controversy, since the breach delivery resulted in the partial paralysis of his left arm and damage to the balance mechanism in his ear. These 'physical' problems have prompted great speculation about the possible psychological consequences upon the young prince. Close attention has also been paid to the strained relationship with his parents, especially his mother. Certainly, he grew apart from them during his adolescent years. He opposed their liberal sympathies and he despised his father's deference to his strong-willed mother. Instead, he preferred the company of his grandfather and the Bismarcks and found solace in the regimental life of the military garrison at Potsdam.

Interpreting the Kaiser's personality remains an issue of great dispute. He was intelligent and at times absolutely charming. He had a broad range of interests and took great pride in his country and ancestry. However, his understanding of issues was usually superficial and distorted by his own personal prejudices. Above all, he was so sensitive to criticism and so taken up by his own self-importance that his moods and behaviour were liable to wild fluctuations. His closest friend, Prinz Philipp zu Eulenburg, whilst on a North Sea cruise with his sovereign in 1900, expressed his concern in correspondence with Bernhard von Bülow, later chancellor:

1 H.M. is no longer in control of himself when He is seized by rage. I regard the situation as highly dangerous and am at a loss to know what to do ... These things cut me to the quick. I have had so much faith in the Kaiser's abilities - and in the passage of time! - Now 5 both have failed, and one sees a person suffering whom one loves dearly but cannot help.

Subsequent profiles have suggested that the Kaiser's behaviour can be seen as symptoms of insanity, megalomania or sadism. More recently, it

Wilhelm II in the uniform of the Garde de Corps *(1901)*

has been suggested that he was narcisstically disturbed, a repressed homosexual or a sufferer from Attention Deficiency Disorder - a mental condition which reveals itself in volatile and irrational behaviour. Clearly, it is difficult to be definitive in such matters, but the consensus now strongly suggests that Wilhelm II was 'if not clinically insane, at least deeply disturbed' (Röhl). However, despite the additional insight given by all these psychological and physiological observations and explanations, the historian must still try to decide the extent to which this personality actually 'shaped' the history of imperial Germany.

Wilhelm II once boasted that he had never read the constitution of the Second Reich. Bearing in mind the complexities of Bismarck's constitutional arrangements his failure to do so was perhaps understandable. However, the anecdote is an interesting insight into the outlook of Germany's sovereign. He had no doubts about his position: he was an autocrat and his authority was based on the divine right of kings and his accountability was to God alone; he was also a Hohenzollern and as such, a warrior king who led and commanded his people militarily. In 1891 he spoke to some new recruits as follows:

1 Recruits! You have sworn Me allegiance. That, children of My Guard, means that you are now My soldiers. You have given yourselves over to Me body and soul. There is only one enemy for you and that is My enemy. With the present Socialist agitation, it 5 may be that I shall order you to shoot down your own families, your brothers, yes, your parents - which may God forbid - but then too you must follow my orders without murmur.

Of course, it is true that the constitution did indeed grant the emperor extensive powers, but his ignorance of its other aspects was a dangerous delusion and self-deception. His desire to establish 'personal rule' was made possible by his monopolistic control over appointments to the imperial government (he of course also enjoyed the same right over the Prussian administration). Bismarck had at least given the system a degree of unity and direction, but the Kaiser possessed neither the character nor the aptitude to be his own chancellor and his leadership amounted to little more than whimsical flights of fancy and blundering interventions. Such inadequacy, however, was perpetuated by his rights of patronage and appointment. By this means the Kaiser was able to surround himself at court and in government with men who were prepared to bolster his own inflated opinion of himself by sympathising with his views. In this sense it is perhaps possible to speak of the Kaiser's 'personal rule'.

The thesis of the Kaiser's 'personal rule' as a system of government centred on the imperial court has been most forcibly argued by the historian John Röhl. Following extensive research, especially amongst the private correspondence of leading figures, he has built up a psychological portrait of the Kaiser to complement his analysis of Wilhelmine politics. He concludes that the essential traits of the Kaiser's 'persona' do equate with those of a mentally unbalanced character. The Kaiser's usual mood could only ever be termed 'manic' and on occasions it turned to 'counter-phobic rage'. Röhl goes on to argue that this neurotic character, flattered and charmed by an inner circle of friends, advisers and military officers successfully established a political primacy over other sources of power. At the centre of this 'system' were the two mutual friends, Eulenburg and Bülow. Eulenburg and the Kaiser were undoubtedly very close. The Kaiser spoke of him as his only 'bosom friend', and Eulenburg 'loved [the Kaiser] above everything else'. Bülow's relationship with the Kaiser was also a close one, but he was sycophantic and insincere, tailoring his letters and conversations to satisfy Wilhelm. This was a successful strategy and though in the end he achieved his aim and became chancellor. In 1898 he wrote to Eulenburg in apparently unambiguous terms:

1 I grow fonder and fonder of the Kaiser. He is so important!! Together with the Great King and the Great Elector he is by far the most important Hohenzollern ever to have lived. In a way I have never before seen he combines genius - the most authentic and 5 original genius - with the clearest *bon sens*. His vivid imagination lifts me like an eagle high above petty detail, yet he can judge soberly what is or is not possible and attainable. And what vitality! What a memory! How quick and sure his understanding! In the Crown Council this morning I was completely overwhelmed!

Röhl's analysis has unashamedly placed individual personality at the very centre of his interpretation of Wilhelmine Germany. However, before looking at other alternative sources of power and influence, it is worth bearing in mind several points. The Kaiser's grasp of politics was limited. Moreover, he was essentially lazy and pleasure-seeking. He was never able to settle down to the regular routine required of government and administration. He much preferred to spend his time playing the social and ceremonial roles of a monarch. He liked to travel and to take part in military manoeuvres - and thus he was actually absent from Berlin for long periods. The Kaiser may have appeared and behaved as an omnipotent autocrat, but was his claim that 'there is only one Ruler in the Reich and I am he' perhaps just another example of his own delusion of power? It is important therefore that the history student strives to distinguish between the projected images of the time and the historical reality.

b) The Emperor and his Chancellors

If Wilhelm II was incapable of governing the country alone, the onus initially fell upon his appointed chancellor. However, none of Bismarck's successors were able to take up the mantle of leadership with any kind of real authority and conviction. Why was this? The short-lived chancellorship of General Leo von Caprivi (1890-4) is proof enough that good intentions, integrity and a conciliatory approach did not suffice in the political environment of Wilhelmine Germany. Ironically, having been appointed in 1890 by Wilhelm II in order to oversee the legalization of Germany's socialists - the party had been outlawed under Bismarck - Caprivi felt obliged to resign in 1894 when his master demanded the drafting of a Subversion Bill directed against the very same party. He was succeeded by Prince Hohenlohe (1894-1900) - an elderly Bavarian aristocrat. His reputation for indecision and procrastination offered exactly the kind of weak leadership which allowed others to exercise influence. Hohenlohe was soon reduced to little more than a figure-head, so that even before Bülow became chancellor (1900-9) the latter had come to exert the more powerful political influence as foreign minister (1897-1900). In December 1897 Bülow wrote to Eulenburg:

1 I am putting the main emphasis on foreign policy ... Only a
successful foreign policy can help to reconcile, pacify, rally, unite.
Its preconditions are of course, caution, patience, tact, reflection ...
It is not a good idea to sound a victory fanfare before the definitive
5 victory, excessive sabre-rattling annoys without frightening.

Another political observer, the Württemberg ambassador, commented on Bülow's political tactics in slightly different terms:

1 I alone have reason to assume that Herr von Bülow, in refraining
from closer contact with the individual *Reichstag* parties, is
pursuing a well-considered intention not to become involved in the
economic and social questions of the state, but, as far as possible,
5 to limit himself and to concentrate on his department of foreign
policy - partly because this alone already lays total claim to his
physical and mental powers, partly too in order not to eclipse
completely the *Reich* chancellor - last not least, in case he himself is
called upon to take his place, in order to keep himself intact
10 *vis-a-vis* the parliamentary parties and not use himself up
prematurely.

A year later Bülow did become chancellor and for nearly a decade he successfully combined the roles of courtier and Chancellor. He kept the affection and trust of the Kaiser and he effectively handled the *Reichstag*.

However, Bülow's domination from 1897-1909 should not be mistaken for genuine authority and purpose. Bülow was a manipulator, whose main concern was to further himself. He thought that this could best be achieved by pandering to the emperor. Eventually, when he failed to show sufficient loyalty to the Kaiser during the '*Daily Telegraph* Affair' (see page 34), he lost that all important prop and his removal soon followed. Germany's last chancellor before the First World War was Bethmann-Hollweg (1909-17), a hard-working and well-meaning bureaucrat, whose virtues were unfortunately not really suited to the demands of the situation. At a time of growing international tension between the great powers his lack of experience in foreign affairs and his ignorance of military issues were highly significant.

Germany's four chancellors in this period differed markedly in character and background. Yet, none of them was ever really able to dominate the German political scene decisively. It is tempting, therefore, to portray their weaknesses and limited political experience as fundamental to the problems of government. This would be an over-simplification. Imperial Germany got the chancellors it deserved. They were the products of a constitution which made them accountable first and foremost to the sovereign. Under Wilhelm I this had not mattered since he had deferred to Bismarck, but his grandson was determined to participate in the affairs of state. Political survival for Germany's four chancellors was therefore essentially dependent upon showing loyalty to the Kaiser and this was far from easy when Wilhelm II's personal involvement was often erratic and blundering.

c) The *Reichstag*

The problems of government in the years after 1890 were also made more difficult by the constitutional arrangements for the Reichstag. Bismarck had always been obliged to secure the support of the Reichstag for government legislation and by one means or another he had usually managed to achieve that. This task had been facilitated by the introduction of anti-socialist legislation in 1878, which had limited the left-wing to a handful of seats. But after 1890 the balance of power in the *Reichstag* shifted significantly. What were these changes in political representation and what were their implications?

On most issues (and there are some important exceptions referred to in the next chapter) the Kaiser and his governments could nearly always rely on the backing of the right-wing parties - the Conservatives, the Free Conservatives and the National Liberals. However, the voting strength of these parties was in decline. In 1887 they gained 48 per cent of the popular vote and 55 per cent of the seats in the *Reichstag* (220): by the time of the last pre-war election of 1912 their share of the vote was down to 26 per cent which in turn gave them only 26 per cent of the *Reichstag* seats (102). The traditional base of support for imperial government was

Major Political Parties in the Wilhelmine *Reichstag*

SPD   *Sozialdemokratische Partei Deutschlands.* Social Democratic
Party.
The party of theoretical Marxism. Closely connected with the
trade unions and supported by the working classes. Proscribed by
anti-socialist legislation from 1878-90, it grew rapidly thereafter.

ZP   *Zentrumspartei.* Centre Party.
Formed in 1871 specifically to uphold the interests of the Catholic
Church and its members from the excesses of Protestant Prussia.
Its appeal was therefore denominational rather than class-based.
Despite the *Kulturkampf* (Bismarck's anti-Catholic policy of the
1870s) it had become an influential political voice in the *Reichstag*.

DKP   *Deutschkonservative Partei.* German Conservative Party.
The party of the landowning farming community. Its outlook was
ultra-conservative and distinctly hostile to the new forces of
political and economic liberalism. Especially strong in Prussia.

RP   *Reichspartei.* Free Conservative Party.
Although conservative in outlook, it was backed by both
industrialists and landowners. Geographical base of support was
not so narrow as DKP.

NLP   *Nationalliberale Partei.* National Liberal Party.
Traditionally the party of economic and political liberalism. It
represented bankers and industrialists and was increasingly
conservative in its policy.

DFP   *Deutsche Freisinnige Partei.* German Free Thought Party (Left
Liberals).
Formed in 1884 following the secession of the more radical
elements from the NLP. It attracted support from progressive
intellectuals and certain elements of the commercial and
professional middle class. In 1893 it split into three factions and
was only re-united in 1910 under the new name of the FVP,
Fortschrittliche Volkspartei, Progressive People's Party.

National Minorities.
The independence parties of the ethnic minorities in Germany.
Poles, Danes, French in Alsace-Lorraine and Guelphs (Hano-
verians).

Right-Wing Splinter Parties.
There were a number of ultra-conservative parties, which were
nationalistic, anti-socialist and often anti-Semitic.

slowly eroded in this period which inevitably exacerbated the problem of finding majority support for the ratification of legislation. In this situation the political stance taken by the Left Liberals, the Centre Party and the Social Democrats (and to some extent the Nationalities) became increasingly important. The Left Liberals, though supportive of the government at times, were generally more critical. However, from 1893 they were divided into at least three factions and were incapable of exerting a decisive voice in the *Reichstag*. The same could not be said of the Centre Party. Its status had been enhanced during Bismarck's *Kulturkampf* and thereafter it consistently won between 90 and 110 seats which made it the largest party in the *Reichstag* - a pre-eminence it continued to hold until the election of 1912. Although its denominational base disguised a wide spectrum of socio-political views ranging from reactionary conservatism to progressive social reform, its parliamentary numbers were such that the Centre Party enjoyed a pivotal role in German politics, as even Bismarck had been forced to recognise. It exploited this position by a pragmatic approach to the parliamentary process, which at times led to fulsome co-operation and accommodation and at others to clear-cut opposition. The Centre Party deputies therefore could not be taken for granted and the imperial government ignored their views at its peril.

Even more significant was the meteoric rise of the Social Democrats as a parliamentary force. Strengthened by the years of persecution, but liberated by the lapse of the anti-socialist laws in 1890, the Social Democratic Party then organized itself into a nationwide mass party. At the Erfurt Congress of 1891 the party adopted an uncompromising Marxist programme to overthrow the Wilhelmine class system. It proved to be a popular manifesto. In 1887 the Social Democrats had polled 10.1 per cent of the vote and gained 2.8 per cent of the seats (11): in 1912 the respective figures were 34.8 per cent and 27.7 per cent (110). And yet, although the party had mobilized the bulk of the working classes behind its banner, there existed very clear divisions within its ranks about how to achieve its aims. Many of the rank and file, especially the trade unionists, came to believe that a policy of 'gradualism' or 'reformism' was the best way to create a socialist society. According to this view, basic parliamentary reforms in living and working conditions represented practical progress towards improving the lot of working people. Such ideas were anathema to traditional Marxists for they involved co-operation and compromise with the bourgeois establishment. The division between reformist and revolutionary socialists was philosophically an important one, but it does not seem to have substantially weakened the electoral appeal of the Social Democrats before 1914. In theory the party remained committed to a revolutionary transformation of society, but in practice many of the deputies in the *Reichstag* were content to talk the rhetoric of revolution whilst working for social and political change through the existing system. Such moderation, however, was on the whole not recognised by the opponents of the Social Democrats. The party was seen as a force for evil, which had to be isolated and controlled - there was no question of embracing it in the process of government.

Reichstag Election Results, 1887-1912

Party	1887	1890	1893	1898	1903	1907	1912
German Conservatives	80	73	72	56	54	60	43
Free Conservatives	41	20	28	23	21	24	14
National Liberals	99	42	53	46	51	54	45
Centre	98	106	96	102	100	105	91
Left Liberals	32	76	48	49	36	49	42
Social Democrats	11	35	44	56	81	43	110
Minorities	33	38	35	34	32	29	33
Right-Wing Splinter Parties	3	7	21	31	22	33	19
Total	397	397	397	397	397	397	397

The balance of political forces in the Wilhelmine *Reichstag* was crucial to Germany's political and constitutional problems at the start of the twentieth century. The *Reichstag* itself was polarized between those who wished to see no change in the existing order and those who desired the creation of a genuine parliamentary democracy in which the imperial government was directly responsible to the *Reichstag* (and not to the Kaiser). This may not have presented any problems if the conservative forces had been able to maintain some sort of majority. However, the gradual decline in their own electoral fortunes, combined with the strength of the Centre Party and the phenomenal rise of the Social Democrats only served to exacerbate profoundly the problem of finding majority support for the ratification of legislation. Moreover, by 1914 this situation showed no sign of resolution since the constitution made no real provision for evolution and adaptation to meet changing circumstances.

3 Political Forces within Wilhelmine Germany

a) The Elites

The problems caused by the Wilhelmine political system have led many German historians to shift the emphasis of their analysis of the *Kaiserreich* away from the political centre. The so-called 'structuralist' school of historiography emerged in the mid-1960s in the wake of the Fischer controversy (see page 41) and it sought to explain history through a detailed examination and synthesis of social, political and economic forces. Foremost amongst the exponents of this methodology is H.U. Wehler.

Wehler and his fellow 'structuralists' have scoffed at the idea of Kaiser Wilhelm II as a dominant influence in the direction of policy and political affairs. They have argued that, whereas Bismarck had provided a focal point for co-ordination, the Kaiser had neither the ability nor the strength of character to do so. In addition they have claimed that, as both the office of chancellor and the institution of the *Reichstag* were restricted by constitutional constraints, there developed a power vacuum after 1890 which created a 'permanent crisis of the state behind its facade of high-handed leadership'.

Wehler has suggested that in this situation other forces were able to emerge and to exert a dominating influence over the nation's affairs. By 'other forces' he meant Prussia's traditional elites: the landowning *Junkers;* the officer class of the army; the professional body of administrative bureaucrats; the judiciary; and the officials of the diplomatic corps. He argued that these non-elected elites were able to exercise power because the imperial constitution had deliberately allowed for the domination of Prussia over Germany's other states. Such a situation might possibly have been able to prevail, if Germany had remained frozen in its social and economic mould of 1871. But, of course, it did not. Germany was in the process of rapid change and new social forces were emerging, most notably an economically powerful entrepreneurial middle class and a class-conscious workers' movement. It was the desire of the traditional elites to maintain their power against what was seen as the threat of genuine mass democracy which prompted them to seek an alliance with the newly emerging elites of industry and commerce by offering them a stake in the system: for example, the provision of armaments contracts and colonial markets overseas. This strategy of rallying together the dominant social elites to protect their own power and status has been dubbed *Sammlungspolitik,* literally 'policy of concentration'. It was supplemented further by deliberately disregarding the forces of democracy and socialism and portraying them as unpatriotic enemies of the Reich. In the view of Wehler, therefore, Germany's decision in the 1890s to undertake *Weltpolitik,* a world policy, was no more than 'social imperialism'. It was simply an attempt to buttress the position of the elites at the top of Germany's class system by diverting the masses away from social and political reform and towards a populist acceptance of the Kaiser and the *Kaiserreich.*

Wehler's 'structuralist' analysis has exerted enormous influence on our understanding of the *Kaiserreich,* though his views have also generated much criticism. Does the manipulation theory exaggerate the unity of purpose within the elites? Was social imperialism really the primary purpose of naval construction? Or was it perhaps merely a desirable side effect? What is the evidence to support the thesis that the elites viewed the naval expansion as an integral part of achieving a

Sammlungspolitik? Such fundamental questions of Wehler's interpretation show that his thesis should not be viewed as an infallible orthodoxy. Equally, however, any student of this period cannot now fail to recognise that the role of the elites is vital to our understanding of Germany's domestic and foreign policies; they must be examined closely as part of any analysis of Imperial Germany.

b) Popular Movements

Structuralist theories and the concepts of 'social imperialism' and *'Sammlungspolitik'* which held such sway in the 1970s have now come to be questioned - especially by a new generation of British and American historians. They have particularly criticised the methodology of structuralism, claiming that it creates a theoretically attractive interpretation which at times cannot be convincingly substantiated by the evidence, or is only supported by selecting the suitable evidence. Some of these critics, like Röhl, not surprisingly, have been unable to accept the reduced role accorded to the Kaiser by the structuralists. Others have claimed that structuralist interpretations concentrate excessively on the elites of German society and thereby ignore other important elements.

Historians, like Blackbourn and Eley, have emphasized the need to get away from the political apex and to look at 'history from below', so as to recognise the importance of popular movements in re-shaping politics at the end of the nineteenth century. In their view the elites lacked any real unity of purpose and therefore they struggled to come to terms with the social foment which accompanied the tremendous economic changes in Germany at this time. Their research has not only focused on the labour, *Mittelstand* and agrarian movements, but also on the non-Prussian regions and the influence of political Catholicism. They have tried to shift the historical emphasis away from Prussia and its elites and instead show that the *Kaiserreich* was a state of many regions with very different political and cultural traditions. Many of these interest groups were asserting rights of political recognition and demanding a genuine voice for the first time, particularly in the wake of the relatively depressed years before 1895. In this way Blackbourn and Eley have successfully highlighted the tremendous growth in political activity in the *Kaiserreich* and also its diversity. This, in turn, has led them to suggest more controversially that Germany's political leaders were not so much manipulating, but actually responding to public opinion. If this was indeed the case then the policies of Wilhelmine Germany were the result of a rather more complex political interaction of forces than previously credited.

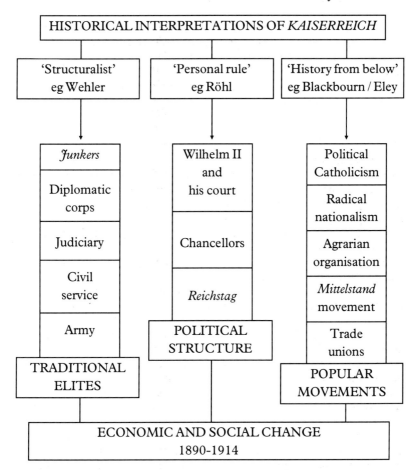

HISTORICAL INTERPRETATIONS OF *KAISERREICH*		
'Structuralist' eg Wehler	'Personal rule' eg Röhl	'History from below' eg Blackbourn / Eley

Junkers	Wilhelm II and his court	Political Catholicism
Diplomatic corps		Radical nationalism
Judiciary	Chancellors	Agrarian organisation
Civil service	*Reichstag*	*Mittelstand* movement
Army	POLITICAL STRUCTURE	Trade unions
TRADITIONAL ELITES		POPULAR MOVEMENTS

| ECONOMIC AND SOCIAL CHANGE 1890-1914 |

Summary - The Structure of Wilhelmine Germany

Making notes on *'The Structure of Wilhelmine Germany'*

The aim of this chapter is to help you to gain a 'feel' for the period, and you should see it as complementing very closely the next chapter which looks at the actual policies of Wilhelmine Germany. You need to gain an appreciation of the major political, economic and social forces at work and the beginnings of an understanding of how it has been interpreted by different historians. There is probably no need for over-detailed notes, but you may feel that you want to come back to this chapter again after reading the next one. The following headings and sub-headings should provide a suitable framework.

1. Economic and Social Change
1.1 The economy. List and explain all the reasons for Germany's economic strength by 1914.
1.2 Society. List and explain the major social effects of such rapid economic development. Look at your notes in the above two sub-sections and compile a list of links between the economic and social changes.
2. The Wilhelmine Political System
2.1 The Kaiser and his court. In about 100 words write a brief character sketch of the Kaiser.
2.2 The chancellors. Compile a list of all the chancellors with dates and explain why each one was appointed and why each one was dismissed.
2.3 The *Reichstag*. Study the table on page 24. Write an 'election analysis' (you could do this either by considering each election in turn or by considering the fortunes of one party at a time). Re-read your notes on the above three sub-sections. Find out from other books how Germany's constitution varied from that of Britain in 1900.
3. Political Forces in Wilhelmine Germany
3.1 The elites. Who were they and how did they exert power?
3.2 Popular movements. What were they and how did they begin to exert influence at the end of the nineteenth century?

Having compiled your notes under the above three main headings, you should be aware that there are three main historiographical trends. Make certain you can explain each one in your own words. At this stage in your study of the *Kaiserreich,* which do you find the most convincing and why?

Source-based questions on 'The Structure of Wilhelmine Germany'

1 Economic and Social Change
Study carefully the tables on pages 11-12. Answer the following questions.
a) Explain the terms 'visible balance' and 'invisible balance'. (2 marks)
b) By reference to the tables on pages 11 and 12 comment on how and why German society changed in the years 1871-1913. (5 marks)
c) Can you suggest any possible reasons why Germany was able to overtake Britain in the production of steel, but not of coal, in the years 1871 to 1910? (3 marks)
d) What questions should an historian ask about the evidence when examining such statistics? (4 marks)
e) To what extent do the facts contained in the tables adequately explain why Germany underwent such rapid economic growth and development in the years 1890 to 1913? (6 marks)

2 Images of the Kaiser
Study carefully the photograph of the Kaiser on page 17. Read also the letter from Eulenburg to Bülow on page 16 and Wilhelm II's speech on page 18. Answer the following questions.
a) What do you think the photographer was attempting to communicate about Wilhelm II in the picture? (5 marks)
b) In what ways do you think the letter and the speech agree in what they imply about the Kaiser's character? (4 marks)
c) Examine the strengths and weaknesses of each source as evidence of the Kaiser's personality. (4 marks)
d) How far do these sources and other evidence known to you support the thesis that Wilhelm II was 'unstable and irresponsible'? (7 marks)

3 The Rise to Power of Bülow
Study carefully the letters of Bülow to Eulenburg on pages 19 and 20 and the report of the Württemberg ambassador on page 20. Answer the following questions.
a) According to the second letter what did Bülow claim his political aims to have been? In what ways does the ambassador's report give a different impression? (4 marks)
b) What do you think Bülow aimed to achieve by expressing his opinions so openly to Eulenburg? (4 marks)
c) What is the value of the ambassador's report to a biographer of Bülow? (4 marks)
d) It has been suggested that Bülow was 'an ambitious and scheming courtier'. How far do these extracts and other evidence known to you substantiate this view? (8 marks)

CHAPTER 3

The Policies of Wilhelmine Germany, 1890-1914

Although this chapter considers in a rather conventional way Imperial Germany's domestic politics and then proceeds on to foreign affairs, it would be wrong to treat the two aspects in isolation. The controversies raised by the historiographical debate about the structure of the *Kaiserreich* have tended to underline the close relationship between economic developments, political tensions at home, foreign and imperial policies, government finances and military/defence strategy. It is important therefore to recognise these links and to realise how these various elements interacted, particularly as some historians maintain that Germany's political leadership deliberately pursued a policy of war in 1914 in an attempt to 'escape' from the state's internal contradictions.

1 Where did Power Really Lie? Domestic Affairs, 1890-1914

a) Caprivi's 'New Course'

If Wilhelm II had assumed that Bismarck's departure would give him a free hand, he was to be initially disappointed. The new chancellor, Caprivi, proved to be more astute and independent-minded than the Kaiser had bargained for Caprivi soon embarked on what he referred to as a 'new course', which involved a more consultative approach to government and a conciliatory attitude to previously hostile forces, such as the Centre Party and the Social Democrats. In contrast to the stalemate between Bismarck and the *Reichstag* in the late 1880s, Caprivi was able to depend on a fair degree of backing from the *Reichstag* to push through a number of social measures in 1891, such as the prohibition of Sunday work and limitations on child and female labour. Such success paved the way for an even more important change - the reform of Germany's tariff policy. Ever since 1879 Germany had upheld a policy of protection for both agriculture and industry. However, prompted by short-term wheat shortages, which had led to a marked rise in food prices, and by the need to stimulate German manufacturing exports, Caprivi negotiated a series of bilateral commercial treaties with Austria-Hungary, Italy, Russia and a number of smaller states between 1891 and 1894. In essence these agreements allowed for a reduction in German tariffs on agricultural goods in return for favourable rates for German manufactured goods. They therefore not only acted as a vital spur to the growth of the German economy, but they also represented a singular political triumph for Caprivi. His policy of tariff reform gained a broad spectrum of support, as most parties, except the Conservatives, recognised the benefits of lower food prices. It seemed as if the new chancellor could perhaps make the Bismarckian system work in a flexible and progressive fashion. It was not to last.

Wilhelm II had initially stood by Caprivi's policy in the belief that kindness would kill socialism. Indeed, the Kaiser had been so taken by the success of the tariff reform that Caprivi had been given the noble title of count. However, the voices of reaction at court had been alienated by Caprivi's 'socialistic' policies and they increasingly encouraged the Kaiser to ditch him and to assume a more authoritarian 'personal rule'. The landowning interest, in particular, which was so well represented in courtly circles, was deeply upset by the commercial treaties since they threatened to reduce their profits. In 1893 the Agrarian League (*Bund der Landwirte* - BdL) was formed to act as an extra-parliamentary pressure group and it demanded all manner of economic privileges for landowners. It quickly grew into an effective and well-organised lobby of a quarter of a million members which acted as a powerful pressure group on behalf of the Conservatives. There had also been resentment in military circles in 1892-3, when Caprivi had made concessions to the *Reichstag* by reducing the length of conscription from three to two years in the Army Bill.

Conservative opposition to Caprivi's 'new course' reinforced Wilhelm II's developing doubts about his chancellor's political suitability, and in 1894 events came to a head. Frightened by a series of anarchist outrages throughout Europe and worried by the success in the previous year of the Social Democrats who increased their total number of seats to 44, Wilhelm II pressed Caprivi to draw up an anti-socialist Subversion Bill. The chancellor's refusal only resulted in the even more extraordinary plan by Wilhelm II and Eulenburg to set aside the powers of the *Reichstag*, crush socialism and establish a more authoritarian system centred on the Kaiser himself. This was the final straw for Caprivi. He successfully talked the Kaiser out of such a course of action, but he had lost the will to carry on.

In October 1894 Caprivi resigned and gladly retired from the political scene. His four years as chancellor neatly encapsulate the difficulties of reconciling the complex and contradictory pressures of the various political forces in imperial Germany. In his attempt to create a genuine base of parliamentary support for the government, Caprivi was appreciating the need in a modern industrial society for a political approach which at least recognised the basic concerns and aspirations of the mass of the population. However, Caprivi's 'new course' foundered, for it alienated the traditional forces of power and influence. He was subjected to considerable abuse from the conservative press; he was the focus of opposition intrigue at court; and in the end, he could not rely on the consistent support of the Kaiser whose *folie de grandeur* was now taken up with thoughts of 'personal rule' and *Weltpolitik*.

b) The Advent of *Weltpolitik*

Although the office of chancellor was held until 1900 by the aged Hohenlohe, government was increasingly dominated by men who were closely in tune with the direction of policy desired by the Kaiser. Hohenlohe was no match for the intrigue at court and in government circles and by 1897 a clique of key political figures had emerged which sympathised with the Kaiser's wish to embark on what he saw as 'personal rule'. In that year there were three new appointees: Admiral von Tirpitz, as navy secretary; Count Posadowsky-Wehner, as interior minister; and above all Bülow, as foreign minister. In addition, two long serving figures began to assume even greater prominence: Friedrich von Holstein, a senior official in the Foreign Office; and Johannes von Miquel, Prussian Finance Minister (and leader of the National Liberals). The emergence of this government team has led many historians to view 1897 as an important turning-point in German history for it coincided with the drive to achieve world power status for Germany by espousing *Weltpolitik* - colonial annexations, the creation of economic spheres of influence and the expansion of naval power to complement the strength of the army (see also page 43). This not only marked a decisive shift in the emphasis of Germany's foreign policy, but also raised all manner of implications for the future of German domestic politics.

How and why did *Weltpolitik* emerge as government policy? Certainly, the Kaiser himself believed in Germany's destiny to become a world power and in the government team assembled in 1897 he had a number of like-minded ministers. However, there were also powerful forces at work in Germany at large which contributed to the new policy. Industrialisation had created economic demands for the acquisition of raw materials and markets beyond Europe - and so at a time when European imperialism was reaching its height, any push to extend the German economic sphere of influence necessitated political backing. The ideology of German nationalism was also being perceived in a different way. The idealistic nationalism of unification was giving way to the ideas of Social Darwinism and the unending struggle between nations. In this sense it was believed by some that the survival of Germany as a leading nation-state necessitated a more active world policy. Finally, economic changes and new intellectual currents also contributed to the emergence of new political forces. The 1890s not only witnessed the rise of the Social Democrats, but also a series of populist right-wing movements, which reflected the radicalisation of the peasantry and the *Mittelstand* (see page 26). These radical nationalists formed a series of pressure groups, of which the most infamous was the Pan-German League (*Alldeutscher Verband*, ADV). Such groups were anti-socialist, racist, anti-Semitic, expansionist and inevitably strong supporters of any policy which advanced German power and influence.

They therefore performed a two-fold purpose: on the one hand they popularised the message of *Weltpolitik* and generated a degree of mass support for the policy, and on the other they exerted political pressure on the imperial government to pursue the policy to the full.

Of central importance to *Weltpolitik* was the decision to expand the German navy. The appointment of Tirpitz provided the human instrument to this end, for he not only enjoyed the full confidence of Wilhelm II, but he also recognised the importance of gaining parliamentary support and popular backing for the plans. With these aims in mind, he was instrumental in the creation in 1898 of the Navy League (*Flottenverein*), which portrayed naval expansion as a patriotic national symbol of Germany's new status in the world. Supported by the financial aid of key industrialists it was able to generate a membership of over one million and this solid groundswell of popular opinion in turn strengthened Tirpitz's position in his handling of the *Reichstag*. When he presented the Naval Bills of 1898 and 1900 they were both passed with substantial majorities, particularly because they were supported by the Centre Party.

The introduction of *Weltpolitik* succeeded where Caprivi's 'new course' had run into the sand because it achieved a greater acceptance across the political divide. It successfully rallied both the middle and upper classes and their political representatives in the *Reichstag* behind the crown and the government. In this sense the support of the Centre Party represented an important step forward, since it helped secure an effective majority for the government in the *Reichstag*. *Weltpolitik* to some extent even reconciled the increasingly vociferous mass of the population to the existing order by playing on their feelings of patriotism and loyalty to the crown. And finally, it was a policy which closely coincided with the aspirations of the Kaiser who convinced himself that domestic policy must therefore at last be under his 'personal rule'.

c) Bülow and the Problems of *Weltpolitik*

However, *Weltpolitik* did not prove to be the complete panacea for the problems of government. Far from it, in fact. Bülow - who was made chancellor in 1900 - found government subject to ever increasing pressures, despite the close relationship he enjoyed with the Kaiser. It was not always so easy to maintain a government majority, as was shown most obviously by the political struggle over the renewal of Caprivi's commercial treaties. The Conservatives in conjunction with the Agrarian League had bitterly campaigned against the agreements from the start, whilst the Left Liberals and the Social Democrats remained committed to lower tariffs. In the end the compromise Tariff Law of 1902 restored tariffs to 1892 levels, which was well short of the Conservatives' demands, and it was only carried by a combination of the Centre, the National Liberals and Free Conservatives.

Weltpolitik generated its own problems too. The budget had moved into deficit as the mounting costs of maintaining the army, expanding the navy and running the empire took effect. If all the 'glories' of *Weltpolitik* were to be continued then substantial tax increases had to be introduced. Bülow was astute enough to realise that this was likely to cause a political storm. And so it did. In 1905 he suggested a two-pronged attack on the deficit by proposing an increase in indirect taxes and an inheritance tax. The proposals came to nothing, for the Centre and the Social Democrats voted down the indirect taxes which would have hit the ordinary person most severely, and the Conservatives and their allies weakened the inheritance tax so as to make it financially insignificant. The deficit continued to grow. Meanwhile Bülow's government was also being attacked for its policy in the colony of S.W. Africa, where a native revolt in 1904-5 had been effectively crushed. Subsequent revelations of brutality and incompetence in the administration of the colony encouraged the Centre Party and others to vote against the government's proposal to provide extra money for the colonial administration.

The problems of imperial government in the early years of the twentieth century suggest that Germany was developing into an increasingly sophisticated political organism. New political forces were at work in the country and yet government, which was traditionally in the hands of conservatives showed only a limited capacity to come to terms with these forces. Powerful interest groups, such as the trade unions and the Catholic Church, were no longer prepared to be ignored and they expected their political representatives to make their voices felt in parliament. Economic forces also exerted dynamic new pressures. The problems of the budget and tariff reform reveal clearly the limitations on implementing government policy and how this in turn generated further political pressures. By 1906 it seemed as if Bülow's government, far from controlling events, was increasingly at the mercy of them.

d) The *Daily Telegraph* Affair

Despite these defeats, Bülow retained the support of the Kaiser and in 1907 the government gained a good result in the so-called 'Hottentot' election (named after the rebels in S.W. Africa) by campaigning on a blatantly nationalistic, anti-socialist and anti-Catholic ticket. This enabled Bülow to bring together the Conservatives, Free Conservatives, National Liberals and Left Liberals in a coalition dubbed the 'Bülow bloc'. However, Bülow's triumph could not and did not last. His coalition was an extremely fragile one and the budgetary deficit was an increasingly serious problem. In the winter of 1908-9 the political crisis came to a head, although in a somewhat bizarre fashion. The German public had already been treated to a moral scandal by the revelation that the Kaiser's close friend, Eulenburg, was at the centre of an extensive ring of homosexuals at court, when the *Daily Telegraph* Affair broke (see account below).

The Kaiser's *Daily Telegraph* interview with Colonel Stuart Wortley.

1 As I have said His Majesty honoured me with a long conversation and spoke with impulsive and unusual frankness. 'You English' he said 'are mad, mad as March Hares. What has come over you that you are so completely given over to suspicions quite unworthy of a 5 great nation? What more can I do than I have done? I declared with all the emphasis at my command in my speech at the Guildhall that my heart is set upon peace, and that it is one of my dearest wishes to live on the best of terms with England. Have I ever been false to my word? Falsehood and prevarication are alien to my nature. My 10 actions ought to speak for themselves, but you listen not to them but to those who misinterpret them. That is a personal insult which I feel and resent ...'

'I repeat' continued His Majesty 'that I am a friend of England but you make it hard for me to remain so. My task is not the easiest. 15 *The prevailing sentiment amongst my own people is not friendly to England. I am in a minority* * in my own land but it is a minority of the best elements ...'

'But you will say, what of the German Navy? Is not that a menace to England? Against whom but England is it being steadily 20 built up? If England is not in the minds of those Germans who are bent on creating a powerful fleet, why is Germany asked to consent to such new and heavy burdens of taxation? My answer is clear. Germany is a young and growing Empire. She has a world-wide commerce which is rapidly expanding, and to which the legitimate 25 ambition of patriotic Germans refuses to assign any bounds. Germany must have a powerful fleet to protect that commerce and her manifold interests in even the most distant seas. She expects those interests to go on growing and she must be able to champion them manfully in any quarter of the globe ... Only those powers 30 which have vast navies will be listened to with respect when the future of the Pacific areas comes to be solved, and if for that reason only Germany must have a powerful fleet. It may even be that England herself will be glad that Germany has a fleet, when they speak together on the same side in the great debates of 35 the future ...'

* For the words in italics the German Foreign Ministry recommended instead: 'The prevailing sentiment amongst large parts of the middle and lower classes of my own people is not friendly to England. So I am so to say in a minority.

Wilhelm II's comments generated heated criticism and there were demands in the *Reichstag* for constitutional restraints to be placed on the Kaiser. However, Bülow himself was in a difficult position, since he had actually cleared the article before publication. The delicacy of the constitutional situation is revealed in a letter written in November 1908 by the British ambassador to his foreign secretary:

1 Prince Bülow spoke at some length and in a very depressed tone of the present crisis in Germany. He said that the Emperor meant so well, but the fact was that, as Bismarck had said, there is no longer room for absolutism in Germany. Parliamentary government was 5 with their countless parties, impossible, but what people clamoured for, and meant to have, was constitutional government. Germany was intensely monarchical and this crisis with its unusually hot outcry against the Sovereign, would, he hoped, pass as other similar crises had passed: but nevertheless, the present 10 feeling against the personal influence of the Emperor in public affairs was very strong, stronger than it had ever been before, and it caused him considerable anxiety. There must in fact be a change; he spoke feelingly on the subject, because, as I had perhaps noticed, his position as things were now, was anything but 15 comfortable.

Caught between loyalty to his friend and master and the baying demands of the *Reichstag*, Bülow sided with the latter. He secured a promise from the Kaiser that constitutional formalities would in future be properly respected. Thereafter, the crisis petered out and no constitutional changes ensued. It seemed as if Bülow (he was nicknamed 'the eel') had once again slithered his way out of a tight corner, but the Kaiser's trust in his chancellor had been fatally weakened by these events and when Bülow's budget proposals were rejected in 1909 the Kaiser secured the chancellor's resignation.

The *Daily Telegraph* Affair provides an illuminating snapshot into the power politics of the Wilhelmine age. Bülow had survived for over a decade at the very centre of German politics by playing the part of the old-fashioned courtier with a sound grasp of how to keep the vested interests satisfied. He retained the backing of the Kaiser through flattery and manipulation and he generated broader political support through the grandiose and nationalistic policy of *Weltpolitik*. However, his failure to stand by the Kaiser in the *Daily Telegraph* Affair underlined how vulnerable the office of chancellor still was to the personal whims of the Kaiser. The chancellor remained accountable to the Kaiser alone and not to the *Reichstag*. This was in spite of the fact that there was a growing body of belief that the Kaiser could no longer behave as an absolute monarch, but must conform to certain constitutional formalities. And yet when the opportunity presented itself for constitutional reform the

Divination by Molten Lead
'We'll just see what the future brings forth.'
'Confound it, that looks like a muzzle.'

Reichstag showed a marked reluctance to assert itself and its authority.

e) Stalemate

In the last few years of peace the German government was nominally in the hands of Chancellor Bethmann-Hollweg. However, his capacity to rule was constrained by powerful circumstantial forces, and between 1909 and 1914 he recoiled from major initiatives. It seemed as if German government had reached political stalemate. Why was this?

Bethmann's parliamentary base of support was just too narrow: his essential conservatism aligned him to the right-wing parties, but his search for broader parliamentary backing was always likely to alienate his natural supporters. In this situation Bethmann tended to avoid reliance on any particular group of parties, but this only led him to become unwittingly more influenced by the extra-parliamentary forces of court, bureaucracy and army, particularly the latter. Indeed, it is no coincidence that the intimate civilian clique which had supported the Kaiser's regime was badly dented by the scandals of 1908 and that, as a result, the military entourage assumed an ever more influential role. Craig maintains that 'the militarisation of Wilhelminian society reached its height during the peace-time years of Bethmann's chancellorship'. The *Reichstag* elections of 1912 further exacerbated Bethmann's parliamentary difficulties (see the table on page 24), since there was a distinct shift to the left with the Social Democrats and a united group of Left Liberals winning 110 and 42 seats respectively. In purely arithmetical terms this amounted to virtual deadlock for the German government. In psychological terms it only served to enhance for the forces of conservatism their fears of democratic and socialist revolution.

However, in the long term there was no way to avoid the looming budgetary crisis and in 1912-3 the interdependent problems of imperial finance and defence came to a head. In the wake of the Second Moroccan Crisis (see page 47) the army and the navy both submitted major expenditure plans. The idea of an effective inheritance tax was again proposed as the only feasible means of raising the revenue, but Bethmann baulked at the hostile political reaction and resorted to the stop-gap measure of taxing spirits. In early 1913 Moltke, the Chief of Staff, went further and demanded a second Army Bill to increase its 'peace-time' strength by 20 per cent to 800,000 men in 1914. Such massive increases could only be met by a significant change in the attitude of the *Reichstag*. Fortunately for Bethmann the inheritance tax was on this occasion accepted. The declining international situation undoubtedly acted as a significant stimulus, though the incongruous state of German politics was revealed by the fact that the tax was still opposed by the Conservatives - who supported the military measures - and supported by the Social Democrats - who traditionally rejected military spending, but were keen to set the precedent of a property-based tax!

f) Conclusion

Just before the outbreak of war German domestic politics was rocked by one further crisis, the Zabern Affair, which neatly crystallised the divisions in German politics and society. After a series of disturbances in the Alsatian town of Zabern in 1913 army officers overruled the civilian authorities and arbitrarily arrested a number of locals. Criticism of the army officers was based on the way they had ignored citizens' rights and placed the army above the law, whilst the army defended itself by claiming to be accountable to the Kaiser alone - and he condoned the action. In the *Reichstag* Bethmann, unlike Bülow in 1908, stood by the army and the Kaiser, but the political opposition was intense and the chancellor received a massive vote of no-confidence. For historians like Röhl the Zabern Affair shows how, right up to 1914, the *Kaiserreich* was still dominated by the actions, decisions and personality of the Kaiser and his entourage. The very fact that Bethmann was able to continue as chancellor despite a major defeat in the *Reichstag* is seen as proof enough of how the Kaiser ultimately provided the framework for policy and political decision-making. For the structuralists, however, Wilhelm II was never more than a 'shadow Kaiser' - a front for the dominant elites who were determined to manipulate the system and government policy in order to preserve their own privileged positions. In this interpretation the Zabern Affair is seen as a classic example of how the army was able to preserve its own authority and status despite the huge public outcry at its action. And finally, for those who write 'history from below' the Zabern Affair is clear evidence of how popular pressures were bubbling up and actually setting the political agenda in an attempt to bring about genuine democratic and social change.

The real danger when trying to draw conclusions about the governance of Imperial Germany is that one can be easily drawn into making over-simple generalisations about a period of history which lasted nearly a quarter of a century and is really quite complex. The historical picture was not uniform between 1890 and 1914 and any conclusion should try to recognise the shifting balance between the political forces. This is by no means an easy task and for those students who crave certainty, it should be recognised that a sensitive analysis of the *Kaiserreich* will probably require conclusions of a more tentative nature. What follows is merely one possible interpretation. It should not be viewed as definitive. It is presented in the hope that it will form a basis for further discussion.

It is impossible to cast aside the Kaiser entirely. In a way, it has been suggested, Wilhelm II came to symbolise the paradoxes of the *Kaiserreich*. On the one hand, he was a defender of traditional Prussian monarchical privileges, and on the other he was an enthusiast for technology, new industries and a world role for Germany. His personal influence in the formation of the imperial government enabled him to set the general tenor of government from 1890 to 1914 - he endorsed (or not as the case may be) the parameters of policy. And from 1897 to 1908 his influence was quite marked. This represented the high-point of the Kaiser's 'personal rule' and it coincided exactly with the political supremacy of Bülow who recognised that his own position depended on flattery and the promotion of the Kaiser's personal whims. However, the Kaiser was not an eighteenth-century absolute monarch. He most definitely could not claim, *l'état, c'est moi* (as Louis XIV of France had done). His political power was within a constitutional framework and there existed powerful forces which acted as both influences and constraints. The role of the Prussian elites, for example, was integral to the functioning of Wilhelmine Germany. Bülow recognised their political significance and developed policy as much as possible with due regard to their interests. Caprivi on the other hand had paid the price of alienating them in the early 1890s. Later on, after the Eulenburg and *Daily Telegraph* scandals, when Wilhelm II's personal position was undoubtedly weakened and the international situation grew more tense, the military clique gained an increasingly influential role at court and in government. However, even then one must guard against an overly generalised picture which portrays the elites as manipulating and dominating the whole political system. There were other forces at work which reflected Germany's long-term history of separatism and its more short-term economic and social transformation into a modernised state. Between 1890 and 1914 these forces became an increasingly important factor in the power politics of the time. Consequently, although the balance of power still rested with the forces of conservatism in 1914, it is also clear that their right to govern was under threat and their ability to govern as they would have liked was already being curtailed by the forces of change. The irreconcilable nature of these two sets of forces was the source of great political tension and frustration. By 1914 Imperial Germany was not yet ungovernable, partly because its economic well-being allayed discontent and also because there was still general respect for the monarchy, but it had reached a situation of political stalemate which made for weak and confused government. The *Kaiserreich* was thus a very complex socio-political organism - just as complex as its sovereign's own eccentric personality. As P. Kennedy writes: 'the Kaiser both reflected and inter-meshed with the country's broader problems'.

2 Germany and the Origins of the First World War: Foreign Affairs, 1890-1914

a) The Importance of the Debate

Inevitably any analysis of European foreign affairs in this period is intimately entwined with the events of 1914 and the causes of the First World War. This is particularly true of Wilhelmine foreign policy, since so much attention has been given over the years by politicians and historians to the question of German 'responsibility' in the debate about the origins of the war. Indeed, the so-called War Guilt Controversy has been described as 'the historical controversy *par excellence*'.

A student of Wilhelmine foreign policy is therefore confronted by a major problem: namely that it is only part - albeit a very fundamental part - of a much broader historical debate. This has important implications. Any attempt to focus on German foreign policy in the years 1890 to 1914 could lead to a very warped perspective about the origins of the First World War. By concentrating on Germany there is a danger of exaggerating the centrality of Germany's role and by extension playing down the role ('responsibility'?) of other countries. There is also the possibility that the over-arching themes of nationalism, imperialism and the arms race, which some historians have identified as central to the outbreak of war in 1914, could be devalued. Thus, the topic of Wilhelmine foreign policy must be seen in its broader perspective, although by the very nature of this volume the concentration is on explaining and analysing the German role. For a more rounded discussion of the 'Origins of the First World War', see the companion volume in this series *Rivalry and Accord: International Relations, 1870-1914*.

But why has imperial Germany's foreign policy been such an important area of historical debate over the years. Initially, of course, it was because the Allies insisted on Germany signing the War Guilt Clause (Article 231) in the Treaty of Versailles (see page 87). This prompted an extensive academic debate in the inter-war years, which eventually resulted in a consensus that the Great Powers had stumbled into war because of the system of international relations and that no one country could be blamed for causing the war. It was a comfortable view for many German historians, even more so in the wake of the traumas of national responsibility and guilt raised by the Third Reich and the Second World War. It was not until the early 1960s that the consensus which had settled over the debate on the origins of the First World War broke down. The publication in 1961 of Fritz Fischer's *Griff nach der Weltmacht* (Germany's Aims in the First World War) advanced the thesis that the German government did bear the decisive share of responsibility for the start of war in 1914 because of its unequivocal desire to achieve a German hegemony over Europe. Within German historical circles Fischer's interpretation caused enormous controversy, which at times degenerated into offensive name-calling and acrimonious squabbling. However, Fischer himself was not dislodged from his stand-point and in 1969 he published another book *Krieg der Illusionen* (War of Illusions), in which he suggested that from the time of the Second Moroccan Crisis in 1911 the German leadership pursued a consistent policy with the aim of fighting a European war as a means of achieving world-power status for Germany.

The Fischer thesis prompted a historical controversy whose reverberations continue to be felt and although the divisions and acrimony are now less, there remain fundamental differences of opinion about the motives and direction of Wilhelmine foreign policy. Therefore, there are five key questions which need to be addressed in this section. Firstly, did the break-up of the Bismarckian system after 1890 'set in train the whole chain of calamity that led towards that catastrophe [the outbreak of the First World War]'? Secondly, did the advent of *Weltpolitik* pose a real threat to the European status quo at the turn of the century? Thirdly, why did attempts to bring about an Anglo-German rapprochement fail? Fourthly, how convincing is the evidence that Germany was actually planning a war in the years before 1914? And finally, how far was Germany responsible for the unfolding of events in the summer of 1914?

b) The End of the Bismarckian System, 1890-7: a calamity or merely a reflection of international realities?

After 1871 Bismarck's diplomacy had ensured the isolation of Germany's major continental enemy, France, by upholding the Triple Alliance, seeking friendship with Britain and signing the Reinsurance Treaty with Russia (1887). In the seven years after Bismarck's fall Germany's international position changed dramatically. Caprivi and Holstein believed that the Reinsurance Treaty was incompatible with Germany's other commitments, especially to Austria-Hungary, and so in March 1890 it was allowed to lapse. Such reading of the Reinsurance Treaty may well have been right, but the result was to push Russia into the arms of France: the two powers signed a military convention in 1892, which laid the basis for an alliance in 1894. The Dual Alliance of 1894 made reality that 'nightmare of coalitions', as Bismarck called it, and confronted Germany with the prospect of a two-front war. Such a danger could have been offset by the cementing of some kind of understanding with Britain - as Caprivi genuinely desired - but diplomatic advances in 1894 failed to find a firm basis for a mutual understanding and the negotiations came to nothing. Indeed, only two years later Anglo-German relations went sharply into reverse over the incident of the 'Kruger Telegram', when the Kaiser sent a congratulatory note to the Boer president for upholding the independence of the Transvaal.

At first sight it is tempting to view Germany's changed position by 1897 as one of decline - with control having passed into the hands of a 'second eleven', who had overseen the collapse of Bismarck's diplomatic system and the creation of a set of diplomatic circumstances which set

Germany on the path towards 1914. However, such an analysis, it could be countered, is heavily influenced by hindsight and our knowledge of how events were to unfold in subsequent years. In comparison to the years before 1890 Germany's foreign policy after 1890 might appear inconsistent and lacking in clear direction. But it must be remembered that the Bismarckian legacy was not without blemish. Cracks had already begun to appear in the Bismarckian system - Russo-German relations had already cooled markedly before his dismissal and there were those who saw the Reinsurance Treaty from the start as no more than a temporary expedient with no long-term benefits. Moreover, after 1890 Germany deliberately pursued what Holstein referred to as a 'free-hand' policy in the hope that differences amongst the other powers combined with friendly German overtures would lead to Germany becoming the decisive voice in Europe. By 1897 Germany had allies in Austria-Hungary and Italy, an improved relationship with France, whilst relations with Russia were slowly recovering. And even though Britain had been upset by the Kruger Telegram incident, the fact was that Britain found itself on far worse terms with Russia and France, than Germany. German foreign policy had moved on from the days of Bismarck and although the Franco-Russian alliance posed an important constraint upon Germany's strategic and diplomatic freedom of action, the situation was certainly not disastrous. Germany was still the dominant power on the continent and its foreign policy represented a sensible response to the prevailing international balance of power.

c) The Advent of *Weltpolitik*, 1897-1907: did it really upset the status quo in Europe?

The decision to pursue *Weltpolitik* in 1897 was a vital moment in German history. It has already been seen how this coincided with important changes on the domestic political scene, but it was also an important turning-point in the evolution of German foreign policy - far more so than 1890. *Weltpolitik* meant different things to different people. For some, it meant the creation of a larger overseas empire by the acquisition of colonies, in order to aid further the expansion of the German economy. For others, it was simply a policy to assist German business to penetrate and then establish areas of economic influence in as many parts of the world as possible. A third view, epitomised by the Pan-German League, amounted to nothing less than a racist *Lebensraum* policy of creating German settlements both overseas and to the east.

Such differences of opinion at the time and the fact that these differences were reflected at the highest levels of the German political and economic establishment have inevitably contributed to difficulties of historical interpretation. For Wehler and Berghahn of the 'structuralist' school, *Weltpolitik* was no more than a 'social imperialism', which was essentially a manoeuvre in domestic politics (see page 33). However, Fischer maintains that in 1897 Germany 'embarked on a course aiming at nothing less than parity with the British world empire, if not more'. This coherent push for world hegemony was to be achieved by a multi-faceted policy: the expansion of the navy; the creation of a large colonial empire in Africa (*Mittelafrika*), and the economic subjugation of Europe to Germany's interests (*Mitteleuropa*). *Weltpolitik*, in Fischer's view, was a grandiose plan involving both continental and overseas expansion to attain world power status.

Attractive as Fischer's interpretation may seem there is a danger that it imposes too much shape and order on the direction of German foreign policy in the years after 1897. If Fischer's understanding of *Weltpolitik* is accurate, why then was the policy in reality so confusing and so incoherent? From 1897 to 1907 the real accomplishments of *Weltpolitik* were actually very limited. Certainly, the navy was started and German economic influence was extended into South America, China, the Near East and the Balkans. However, Germany's small and costly empire only gained the Chinese port of Kiaochow (1897) and a few islands in the Pacific (1899). Moreover, the diplomatic and strategic consequences of *Weltpolitik* were disastrous. Bülow and Holstein believed that the policy of maintaining a 'free hand' was consistent with *Weltpolitik:* they believed that Britain and Russia would remain at loggerheads. Thus, little enthusiasm was shown towards British overtures for an alliance between 1898 and 1901. Instead, there was a gradual distancing between Britain and Germany - the result of anti-English feeling prompted by the Boer War and the British perception of the threat posed by the German navy after the second Naval Law. What had not been envisaged though, was the possibility that Britain would allay its developing fears of isolation by signing an alliance with Japan (1902) and an entente with France (1904). The former was only limited to the Pacific arena and the latter was not an alliance - but merely an understanding to settle differences and to encourage future diplomatic co-operation. However, there was no disguising the fact that Britain had been alienated and that Germany could no longer rely on Anglo-French antagonism to strengthen its own hand. It was the desire to break the entente which prompted Germany to provoke the Moroccan Crisis of 1905-6. By claiming to uphold Moroccan independence in a territory which had become a French sphere of influence, Bülow hoped to reveal the flimsy nature of Britain's loyalty to the entente. It was not to be. At the international conference at Algeçiras Germany suffered a major diplomatic defeat. It found itself diplomatically isolated and France got its way over Morocco. The entente had stood firm - indeed under Germany's pressure it had been strengthened. To make matters worse, one year later Britain signed an entente with Russia (1907).

The decision to embark on *Weltpolitik* in 1897 was probably at first no more than a desire broadly felt in Germany that Germany should

The Aims of German Naval Policy

A. Chancellor Hohenlohe introduced the Naval Bill to the *Reichstag* on 6 December 1897:

1 This measure shows you that we are not thinking of competing with the great sea powers, and for those with eyes to see it demonstrates that a policy of adventure is far from our minds. Precisely because we want to carry a peaceful policy, we must make an effort to build
5 our fleet into a power factor which carries the necessary weight in the eyes of friend and foe alike ... In maritime questions, Germany must be able to speak a modest but, above all, a wholly German word.

B. Memorandum of Admiral Tirpitz to Wilhelm II in 1897:

1 ... the most dangerous naval enemy at the present time is England. It is also the enemy against which we most urgently require a certain measure of force as a political power factor ... Commerce raiding and transatlantic war against England is so hopeless, because of the
5 shortage of bases on our side and the superfluity on England's side, that we must ignore this type of war against England in our plans for the constitution of the fleet ... Our fleet must be so constructed that it can unfold its greatest military potential between Heligoland and the Thames ... The military situation against England demands
10 battleships in as great a number as possible.

C. The Austrian Ambassador, Szögényi, in a report of February 1900:

1 The leading German statesmen and above all Kaiser Wilhelm, have looked into the distant future and are striving to make Germany's already swiftly growing position as a world power into a dominating one, reckoning thereby upon becoming the ingenious successor to
5 England in this respect. People in Berlin are, however, well aware that Germany would not be in the position today to assume this succession, and for this reason a speedy collapse of English world power is not desired since it is fully recognised that Germany's far-reaching plans are at present only castles in the air.
10 Notwithstanding this Germany is already preparing with speed and vigour for her self-appointed future mission. In this connexion I may permit myself to refer to the constant concern for the growth of German naval forces ... England is now regarded as the dangerous enemy which, at least as long as Germany is not sufficiently armed
15 at sea, must be treated with consideration in all ways.

somehow 'catch up'. This meant different things to different people: the thinking of the key figures was certainly not identical, but a confusing mixture of hopes, fears and ignorance. There was no real planning or co-ordination and consequently, after ten years of *Weltpolitik* Germany found itself in an ambivalent position. The real benefits of *Weltpolitik* remained limited to the commercial advantages from informal economic penetration overseas and the kudos arising from possessing a powerful army and navy - Germany's colonial possessions remained minimal. In this sense, *Weltpolitik*, at very considerable financial cost, achieved very little towards promoting Germany to world power status and it could therefore be argued (as many Germans did at the time) that the policy did not pose a threat to anyone else. However, *Weltpolitik* was not perceived like this outside of Germany. Britain had been alienated and had therefore determinedly maintained a significant naval lead whilst aligning itself with France and Russia in the Triple Entente. As a result Germany's diplomatic and strategic position was in many respects decisively weaker in 1907 than it had been for a generation or more. In this sense *Weltpolitik* contributed to an important change in the European status quo.

d) 1907-11: Why Did Anglo-German Rapprochement Fail?

By 1907 the major powers of Europe were already divided along lines which would parallel those of 1914. It could be thought that the die was cast. However, such a view is not tenable. The crises in Bosnia (1908-9), Morocco (1911), and the Balkan Wars (1912-3) all passed off without the outbreak of a general continental war. Moreover, it should not be forgotten that genuine efforts were made at this time to put the crucial relationship between Britain and Germany on a sounder footing. And if an Anglo-German entente had been agreed, then the situation in 1914 would have been very different indeed.

　　Anglo-German relations reached a veritable low in 1909, when high-handed German diplomacy in the Bosnian crisis hardened existing doubts within the Triple Entente about the true purpose of German foreign policy. This was especially true in Britain, since it coincided with a renewed concern over the vexed issue of German naval strength. Despite the financial problems faced by the German government (see page 34), Bülow had accepted Tirpitz's proposal of two supplementary naval laws in 1906 and 1908 which amounted to a significant quantitative and qualitative growth in the German navy. Britain was now seriously concerned that British naval supremacy was threatened and that the German navy could logically only be directed against it. The political and public furore in Britain came to a head in 1909 and as a consequence the British government decided to increase naval expenditure substantially in order to maintain Britain's maritime lead. The two countries had become enmeshed in an expensive naval arms race, which was exacerbating further an already uneasy relationship. The appointment of Bethmann as chancellor was followed by an attempt to recover the situation. He recognised that an agreement with Britain to limit naval construction would not only reduce his budget difficulties, but could also loosen Britain's ties to the Triple Entente. There were also powerful people in Britain who saw the advantages of a settlement of Anglo-German differences. Negotiations were carried on between 1909 and 1911. Britain pressed for an actual reduction in German naval strength and Germany demanded a promise of British neutrality in the event of an attack by France or Russia. However, the demands placed by each side on the other were just too much and the gap could not be bridged. The Kaiser and Tirpitz did not seriously envisage any concessions over the fleet and Bethmann was only able to offer a deceleration in construction. Britain in turn viewed the German request for British neutrality as too high a price.

Perhaps, both sides expected too much too soon. Perhaps, with time the negotiations could have laid the basis for an understanding. But in 1911 Germany provoked another diplomatic clash over Morocco. What started as an attempt to extract territorial compensation from the French empire because of France's contravention of the Algeçiras agreement developed into a major Anglo-German dispute, as Britain stood by its entente partner in the face of perceived German bullying. In this situation the German government was not prepared to force the issue and risk war. It backed down and accepted a narrow strip of the French Congo as compensation. Little had been gained by the episode and much had been lost. Political tension between Germany and Britain had been heightened and an increasingly virulent strain of xenophobia began to permeate elements of the press on both sides which pressed for further arms expenditure.

e) 1911-14: Was Germany Planning a War?

The last three years of peace have been the focus of immensely detailed analysis amongst historians examining Germany's role in the causes of the First World War. Fischer maintains that the 'excitement and bitterness of nationalist opinion over what was seen to be the humiliating outcome of the [Moroccan] crisis were profound and enduring'. 1911 marks an important watershed in German foreign policy, he argues, because from that point there existed a clear continuity of German aims and policies which culminated in the war of August 1914.

Central to Fischer's thesis are the events of 1912. The outbreak of the Balkan Wars represented an important de-stabilising factor, particularly as Germany's main ally, Austria-Hungary, was threatened by an increasingly powerful and nationalistic Serbia, which in turn was backed by Russia. This increasing sense of isolation and encirclement was underlined further when, following another failed attempt to find any basis for rapprochement, Lord Haldane (the British - and pro-German - war minister) later stated through the ambassador in London that Britain would stand by France unconditionally in the event of a continental war because it could not allow the balance of power in Europe to be disturbed. The upshot of this was the summoning of a meeting of Germany's army and navy chiefs on 8 December 1912, reports of which can be seen on page 49.

This meeting has become known as the 'War Council' meeting and for supporters of the Fischer school it provides conclusive evidence of German intentions to fight a war, but at a time most suitable to German military and strategic interests. Other historians have not been so convinced. They have highlighted Müller's comments that 'the result amounted to almost nothing'. Attention has also been drawn to the informal nature of the meeting which was not even attended by Bethmann. Perhaps, the meeting was simply another example of a hastily assembled gathering in response to an outburst by the Kaiser. More generally, it has been questioned whether the chaotic nature of Wilhelmine government was actually capable of such clear-sighted long-term planning.

There was definitely a growing mood of pessimism and uncertainty about the future in Germany by 1914. Germany had been drawn into an ever closer dependence upon Austria-Hungary, which increased the possibility of Germany being sucked into the Balkan quagmire, and the early months of 1914 witnessed a sharp deterioration in Russo-German relations. In some influential quarters of the German establishment there certainly prevailed a belief that preventive war provided the only escape from the looming crisis. However, in the last few months of peace Bethmann still saw hopeful signs in Germany's international position. He was encouraged by the extent of Anglo-German co-operation during the Balkan Wars and by the peaceful settlement of several colonial disputes.

To suggest that the evidence proves that the German government was actually planning to unleash a war in the summer of 1914 is to go too far. War plans certainly existed - and the 'War Council' meeting of December 1912 is clear evidence of how war was considered to be a viable option. What it also reveals is that from 1912 German leaders were acutely aware in their own minds of how 1914-15 represented the optimal time for war from the German standpoint. These considerations were surely massively influential when the Sarajevo crisis developed.

f) July 1914: Why did Germany Go to War?

This is not the place for a detailed factual account of the events across Europe in the six weeks after 28 June 1914. Rather, it is more relevant to concentrate on the decision-making process in Germany during this time. Following the assassination of the Archduke Franz Ferdinand the

The 'War Council' Meeting, 1912
A. Diary entry for 8 December 1912 of Admiral Georg von Müller who attended the meeting:

1 Tirpitz made the observation that the navy would prefer to see the postponement of the great fight for one-and-half years. Moltke says the navy would not be even ready then and the army would get into an increasingly unfavourable position, for the enemies were arming
5 more strongly than we, as we were very short of money.
   That was the end of the conference. The result amounted to almost nothing.
   The Chief of the General Staff says: War sooner the better, but he does not draw the logical conclusion from this, which is: To
10 present Russia or France with an ultimatum which would unleash the war with right on our side.

B. Diary entry for 9 December 1912 of Albert Hopman, who had spoken to Tirpitz:

1 His Majesty sees Austria's demands as expressing the vital interests of the Habsburg monarchy which she can on no account give up and which we [Germany] must support. He does not believe that Serbia will knuckle under. The Chief of Staff regards war as
5 unavoidable and says the sooner the better. Tirpitz contradicted him and said it lay in the interests of the Navy to postpone if possible for 1-2 years. The army, too, could do much in the intervening time to make better use of our surplus population.

C. Report of General von Wenniger, Bavarian military envoy in Berlin, 15 December 1912 based upon information from the Prussian war minister, the brother of Vice-Admiral Heeringen, who did attend:

1 A week ago today H.M. summoned Moltke, Tirpitz and Müller (Bethmann, Heeringen [Prussian war minister] and Kiderlen were not invited!) and informed them in a most agitated state that he had heard that ... 'England would stand on the side of Germany's
5 enemies, whether Germany attacked or was herself attacked' ... Moltke wanted to launch an immediate attack; there had not been a more favourable opportunity since the formation of the Triple Alliance. Tirpitz demanded a postponement for one year, until the [Kiel] Canal and the U-boat harbour on Heligoland were finished.
10 He told the War Minister the following day only that he should prepare a new large Army Bill immediately. Tirpitz received the same order for the fleet ... Your Excellency will see that the picture behind the scenes is very different from that on the official stage.

German reaction was initially to give full support to Austria-Hungary and this was done by the so-called 'blank cheque'. However, the German pressure for swift and decisive action combined with German knowledge of the severity of the ultimatum being prepared against Serbia suggests that Germany was pursuing more than just defensive diplomatic tactics on behalf of its ally. Bethmann seems to have recognised that the situation provided a genuine opportunity to assert Austrian power against Serbia in a localised conflict and thereby to score a significant diplomatic victory over Russia (and by extension over the Entente in general). Such a stratagem was of course a gamble, with the risk that Russia would stand by Serbia and thus broaden the conflict. In the first four weeks of July the German leaders seem to have been prepared to take that chance in the belief that Germany would win a continental war. The diary of K. Riezler, secretary to Bethmann provides an illuminating insight:

1 7.7.1914 ... Our old dilemma in every Austrian move in the Balkans. If we encourage them, they will say we pushed them into it; if we try to dissuade them, then we're supposed to have left them in the lurch. Then they turn to the western powers whose arms are
5 open, and we lose our last halfway reliable ally. This time it's worse than 1912; for this time Austria is on the defensive against the subversive activities of Serbia and Russia. A move against Serbia can lead to world war. 23.7.1914 ... The Chancellor believes that if there is war it will be unleashed by Russian mobilisation ... In this
10 case there will be little to negotiate about because we shall have to wage war immediately in order to have a chance of winning. Yet, the entire nation will then sense the danger and rise in arms.

At this stage Germany did not necessarily want war, but it certainly seems to have been prepared to risk it.

The Austrian ultimatum to Serbia on 23 July brought home to the major powers the implications of the crisis. Britain, in particular, tried to mediate by calling for an international conference, but significantly Germany ignored such proposals and privately urged Austria-Hungary to take military action because 'any delay in commencing military operations is regarded as a great danger because of the interference of other powers'. It would seem therefore that until 27 July there was a reasonable degree of unanimity amongst the leaders of Germany, but thereafter doubts began to emerge amongst some of the key figures and divisions over policy ensued. The Kaiser returned from his holiday on 28 July and proposed that the Austrians should 'halt in Belgrade' and then negotiate on the basis of the Serbian reply. On the other hand, Moltke was pressing his opposite number in Vienna for immediate mobilisation. The confusion sown by such contradictory interventions from such key figures was hardly clarified by Bethmann. Bethmann was either pursuing an elaborate diplomatic game to make Germany appear the innocent party in the face of Russian aggression (and thus unite German public opinion behind the war) or he too was having doubts about the wisdom of the high-risk strategy.

The Austrian declaration of war on Serbia on 28 July was followed by a Russian decision to order general mobilisation on 31 July. On the previous day Bethmann had stated at a meeting 'that things are out of control and the stone has started to roll'. The crisis had gone beyond a situation where the considerations of diplomacy were paramount to one where military matters took precedence. In Germany this was reflected by the increasing influence of the generals. Falkenhayn, the war minister, had already tried unsuccessfully to force Bethmann into ordering a pre-mobilisation alert. And Moltke deliberately deceived his own government by urging Austria-Hungary to order general mobilisation against Russia although it had been agreed previously to give Russia another 24 hours to back down. The point here is that Moltke and the generals not only saw the summer of 1914 as a logistically opportune moment, but they also recognised that once Russia had mobilised, Germany was strategically committed to fight. This was the inevitable result of the Schlieffen Plan, drawn up by Moltke's predecessor, which intended to counteract the threat of a two-front war with the Dual Alliance by launching a rapid all-out assault in the west in order to defeat France before turning east to face Russia. Thus, as soon as Russia began to mobilise, Germany had no time to lose in mobilising its own forces. The diplomatic gamble had failed and Bethmann recognised the politico-military imperatives. War was declared on Russia on 1 August and on France on 3 August. By this time there was no realistic hope of Britain remaining neutral. The British ambassador and foreign secretary had both made it clear in the last few days of July that it was not in Britain's interests to stand aside and allow Germany to dominate Europe. Admittedly, the British Cabinet remained divided over intervention until 2 August, but the prospect of Belgian neutrality being violated as part of the Schlieffen Plan, facilitated the decision that Britain too must fight Germany.

g) Conclusion: Germany's Responsibility?

Fischer's interpretation of German foreign policy has been massively influential. But his views and approach, as has been touched upon, have not been without criticism. Berghahn and Wehler, for example, do not deny the essential responsibility of Germany for starting the war. Berghahn bluntly states: 'the historian does not any longer have to undertake a round-trip through the capitals of Europe to locate those primarily responsible. They were sitting in Berlin'. However, the emphasis of the German structuralist school is very much on the profound effects the accumulating domestic pressures in 1913-14 had upon the decision to go to war. The budget deficit, the political power of the Social Democrats and the Zabern Affair are all seen as indicative of a fundamental internal crisis which encouraged the Prusso-German elites to pursue a war policy as a means of deflecting the political opposition and thereby preserving their own threatened position. This is generally referred to as the 'escape forwards' theory. Some critics have gone even further and suggested that the Reich was ungovernable - that it had become 'a polycracy of forces' which counteracted each other and made coherent decision-making an impossibility. According to such an analysis the structure of the *Kaiserreich* was so chaotic that the pursuit of an offensive war policy was effectively beyond the government's capability.

Although the inter-war view of German policy in 1914 as one of 'defensive war' against the Entente is now generally not accepted, some historians have continued to criticise Fischer for over-emphasising Germany's aggressive and expansionist tendencies. It has been suggested that 1914 was an 'offensively conducted defensive war' by Germany - an attempt to break free from the pressures brought about by diplomatic isolation and the threatening power of Russia by a preventive strike. This has most recently been taken further and placed on an even more abstract level by Stürmer, who argues that the exposed geostrategic position of Germany must be seen as one of the vital factors in the making of German foreign policy.

As 1914 recedes further into the past the debate about the war's causes becomes less blurred by the question of 'guilt'. Younger generations detached from the horrors of two world wars have less reason to search for scapegoats - Germany and Britain are now partners in the European Community. However, the search for historical explanations cannot avoid the allocation of responsibility, whether it is placed on individuals or abstractions.

Clearly, one cannot ignore the context of Europe at the turn of the century. Powerful forces - technological, economic, ideological and demographic - were at work which helped to shape the international situation and make the war possible. However, to emphasise the primacy of such long-term factors is dangerously close to suggesting that 1914 was somehow inevitable. An interesting modern comparison might be that all the ingredients existed from the late-1940s to the late-1980s for another worldwide conflict, but the flashpoints of the Cold War *never* did actually develop into World War Three! As J. Röhl has written:

1 To argue that an event had deep causes and profound consequences is surely not to say that the deep causes were *sufficient* in themselves to bring about the event. It is my belief that the deeper causes ... were necessary, certainly, to produce the kind
5 of war which broke out in 1914, but that those deeper factors

(which had after all been present in the European situation for several decades prior to the outbreak of war) did not lead by themselves to a self-activation of war. The deeper causes were *necessary* but not *sufficient*. What is still missing is the decision-
10 making dimension.

When one looks at the evidence from this benchmark, it is difficult to escape from the conclusion that the German leadership must shoulder the major responsibility both for the worsening international atmosphere in the five or so years before 1914 and also for the escalation of the July crisis into a continental war.

German *Weltpolitik* and the ham-fisted diplomacy which accompanied it had contributed to a marked increase in international tension and to a dangerous deterioration in Germany's strategic position by about 1907. However, more significantly, in the following years there was no concerted attempt by Germany to overcome this - no preparedness to compromise as a way to engender conciliation and trust. Instead, German foreign policy was generally typified by a hawkish mentality of bluster and brinkmanship and by an increased determination to stand by Germany's one remaining reliable ally, Austria-Hungary. This policy and approach came to a head in the German response to and direction of events in the July crisis. From early July Bethmann adopted a strategy of calculated risk in the hope of winning a diplomatic victory which would decisively weaken the Entente. To achieve this end the crisis was deliberately escalated and attempts at constructive mediation were torpedoed. All this was done because it was also believed that the failure of diplomacy would lead to a war with the Entente powers, which, according to the assessment of the generals, Germany at that time could win. Thus, when Russia did mobilise Germany willingly accepted the challenge and implemented the Schlieffen Plan.

Making notes on *'The Policies of Wilhelmine Germany'*

As the events described and discussed in this chapter are central to your understanding of the *Kaiserreich*, you should aim to make detailed notes. However, before you start, do the following:

i)   Make certain you are absolutely clear in your own mind about all the elements which contributed to the analysis of the structure of the *Kaiserreich* as detailed in Chapter 2.
ii) Study the summary diagram below and the chronological table on page 156-8. Compile two parallel timelines for domestic and foreign affairs, so as to gain a general overview of the period.

Then, you would be well-advised for this chapter to take notes following exactly the headings and sub-headings in the text. In the first section on domestic affairs you need to bear in mind all the time the question in the sub-title 'Where did power really lie?' and try to recognise the relative significance at each stage of the various political forces. In the second section that question remains very pertinent, but it is over-shadowed by the controversy of Germany's responsibility in the origins of the First World War. Both these questions are of great historical significance and there continues to be important differences of interpretation over them. Therefore, it would be a good idea at the end to write up a sub-section entitled 'What I think' on each of the major issues.

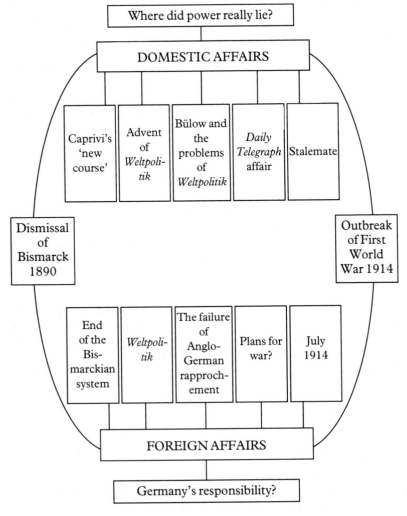

Summary - The Policies of Wilhelmine Germany

Answering essay questions on 'The Policies of Wilhelmine Germany'
You are most likely to be asked very broad essay questions on imperial Germany. It is therefore very important that you establish clearly in your own mind what exactly is the *focus* of any question set. A good way to do this is to ask yourself the following mini-questions.

a) What are the chronological parameters of the question? Does it concentrate on 1890-1914 or perhaps 1890-1918? Does it require reference to imperial Germany pre-1890?

b) What aspects of the period are relevant? Does it focus on one or more of political, social or economic factors? Does it require attention to domestic and/or foreign affairs?

c) Is anything else 'extra' required? Does it perhaps require a knowledge of other countries' history? (This may particularly be the case with foreign affairs.)

This may sound a little mechanical, but it will get you into good habits and if done regularly it will become almost second nature after a while. Look at the following essay questions on imperial Germany and then decide on the focus of each one by using the technique above:

1. What were the strengths and weaknesses of the *Kaiserreich* in 1914?
2. Who ruled imperial Germany?
3. Account for Edward VIII's description of Wilhelm II as 'the most brilliant failure in history'.
4. 'Germany's problems in the period 1890-1914 were not primarily due to the deficiencies of Wilhelm II.' How far do you agree?
5. Why did Germany go to war in 1914?

You probably found that some were quite easy to categorise whilst others left doubts in your mind. If you are uncertain about the focus of a question, you could make use of that uncertainty by turning it into one of your discussion points in the essay. A candidate who shows such a thoughtful approach will usually be well rewarded by an examiner. Alternatively, if you don't feel confident about the focus of a question, it is probably best to leave it well alone and congratulate yourself for not falling into deep water!

Source-based questions on 'The Policies of Wilhelmine Germany'

1 The *Daily Telegraph* Affair
Read the text of the *Daily Telegraph* article and the letter of the British ambassador on pages 35 and 36. Study the cartoon of the Kaiser on page

37. Answer the following questions.
a) With reference to the text explain why the Kaiser's comments generated so much criticism within Germany. (3 marks)
b) What impression is conveyed by the cartoonist about the Kaiser? (4 marks)
c) Why do you think the German Foreign Office amended the text in the way it did? (3 marks)
d) According to the ambassador's letter what was Bülow's response to the crisis? How reliable is this source as evidence of Bülow's reaction? (7 marks)
e) If political hostility was so marked towards Wilhelm II, why did the *Daily Telegraph* Affair not lead to constitutional reform? (8 marks)

2 The Aims of German Naval Policy

Read carefully the three extracts on pages 45. Answer the following questions.
a) In what ways might Germany need a navy 'as a political power factor'? (4 marks)
b) What were the aims of the German navy according to Hohenlohe? What were the aims of the German navy according to Tirpitz? (6 marks)
c) How do you explain the differences in tone and content between sources A and B? (6 marks)
d) How reliable is Szogenyi's report as evidence of German intentions in 1900? (4 marks)

3 The 'War Council' Meeting 1912

Read carefully the three extracts on pages 49. Answer the following questions.
a) Explain the references: (i) 'He does not believe that Serbia will knuckle under' and (ii) 'the formation of the Triple Alliance'. (2 marks)
b) What are the possible explanations for the absence of Bethmann and the foreign minister from this meeting? (5 marks)
c) How reliable a record of the discussions on 8 December 1912 are these sources? (6 marks)
d) With reference to these sources and other evidence known to you, do you believe that Germany was intending to wage war in 1914? (7 marks)

CHAPTER 4

Germany in War and Revolution, 1914-19

There is now little doubt amongst historians that the effects of the First World War were absolutely crucial to Germany's historical development. The war acted as both the stimulus and occasion for change. Germany entered the First World War as a semi-autocracy; four years later in the wake of military defeat the Kaiser himself abdicated and fled to Holland and the *Kaiserreich* gave way to a democracy, the so-called Weimar Republic. Why did Imperial Germany fail to achieve the expected victory and in what ways did the protracted conflict affect the country? Above all, is it correct to describe the changes at the end of the war as amounting to a 'German revolution'? These are the questions which lie at the heart of Germany in war and revolution.

1 Why did Germany Lose the First World War?

a) The Breakdown of the Schlieffen Plan

It is tempting to suggest that Germany's eventual military defeat in autumn 1918 is a classic example of how a long-term factor can prove to be decisive in historical causation. For in this case it seems that Germany's inability to achieve a quick victory in the autumn of 1914 resulted in a war of stalemate for which the country was militarily and economically unprepared and strategically ill-suited.

Germany's military chiefs had long recognised the weakness of Germany's strategic position if confronted by a combined attack on both western and eastern fronts. The Schlieffen Plan, named after the Chief of the General Staff between 1891 and 1906, had been deliberately devised as a means to counter that particular dilemma. In simple terms the plan had envisaged a massive assault in the west through Belgium so as to encircle Paris and defeat France within six weeks. This would then enable the transfer of German troops to the east to confront the forces of Russia which, it was assumed, because of the state's relative backwardness, would take much longer to mobilise.

Although attractive in theory, the final draft of the plan produced by Schlieffen in 1905 was flawed in a number of ways. In order to advance on a broad front the plan quite deliberately violated the neutrality of Belgium, the Netherlands and Luxemburg without regard to the possible political and diplomatic consequences of such actions - yet another indication of the dominating influence of the military in the decision-making process of imperial Germany. And secondly, the plan was framed at a time of severe political and military weakness for Tsarist Russia and consequently, the assumptions about the slow speed of

Russian mobilisation did not necessarily hold good for the future. In addition, Schlieffen's successor, Moltke, made a number of amendments: the advance through the Netherlands was re-routed to prevent Dutch involvement; whilst concern about the strength of the likely French assault in Alsace-Lorraine led him to transfer some forces to the southern flank. Whether the effects of both these changes were decisive in the failure of the plan has long been disputed. What does seem clear is that even before the first shots had been fired the military odds were not in Germany's favour. The Schlieffen Plan did not provide any guarantee of success, and yet its failure was likely to draw Germany into a war which its own generals knew would be highly problematic.

Wilhelm II's Proclamation of 6 August 1914

To the German People

1 Ever since the foundation of our empire it has been the greatest endeavour for me and for my forefathers over the last 43 years to preserve peace in the world and to continue our powerful development in peace. But our enemies envy the success of our
5 work. All the open and secret hostility from east and west and from beyond the sea we have endured conscious of our responsibility and power. But now these enemies want to humiliate us. They wish us to look on with folded arms as they prepare a malicious attack; they do not tolerate our standing side by side in determined
10 loyalty with our allies who fight for their reputations as empires and with their humiliation we will lose our power and honour as well. Therefore the sword must now decide. In the midst of peace the enemy attacks us. Forward. To arms. Every moment of wavering, every hesitation is treason against the Fatherland. The existence or
15 destruction of our re-created empire is now at stake, the very existence of German power and customs. We will resist to the last breath of air of man and horse. And we will win this fight even against a world of enemies. Germany has never lost when it has been united. Forward with God who will be with us as He was with
20 our fathers.
Berlin. 6 August 1914. Wilhelm.

However, the optimism and public euphoria of 4 August 1914 soon came up against military realities. Russia did indeed mobilise more quickly than expected and in desperation Moltke transferred a further two army corps to the eastern front. The main offensive meanwhile came up against stiffer than expected Belgian resistance and then the troops of the BEF (British Expeditionary Force). The momentum of the German advance was lost and it was decided not to encircle Paris. The allies counter-attacked at the battle of the Marne (September 1914) and German forces retreated to the river Aisne. The Schlieffen Plan had failed. Moltke resigned having suffered what amounted to a nervous breakdown and was succeeded by Falkenhayn as the chief of the OHL, *Oberste Heeresleitung,* (Army Supreme Command). Admittedly, Germany had gained a couple of memorable victories against Russia, but Russia was still very much in the war and a very real threat to Austria-Hungary, Germany's major ally.

The implications of Germany's inability to gain the intended quick victory were far-reaching. By November 1914 Germany was confronted with a two-front war - a war which it had always wished to avoid and for which it was not prepared militarily, let alone socially or economically. The generals had long recognised the dangers of such a situation, but in the end their plan had been unable to prevent it. If Germany were to win the war, it had to develop a viable alternative strategy.

b) The Failure of Alternative Strategies

Throughout 1915 Germany struggled to formulate an appropriate long-term strategy to overcome the unexpected military stalemate. Victories on the eastern front against Russia and the withdrawal of the Allies from the Dardanelles campaign could not alter the fact that time was against Germany. The Allies had already gained the maritime advantage by seizing German colonies and destroying its roving cruiser squadron, but most significantly Britain had imposed a naval blockade which severely limited Germany's ability to import. The German response to this threat is telling evidence of the leadership's inability to develop a co-ordinated and purposeful strategy. Tirpitz wanted to engage the British fleet in battle in order to break the blockade. However, other voices felt that this was far too risky. As an alternative, Tirpitz consequently pressed for the use of unrestricted submarine warfare, but this too generated fierce controversy. There were doubts about the morality, as well as the efficacy of the policy. Bethmann was also rightly aware of the possible diplomatic consequences for the neutral USA. However, Bethmann accepted military advice and in February 1915 unrestricted submarine warfare was introduced - it was ended in September following the sinking of the liner *Lusitania.* In February 1916 the policy was re-adopted - only to be dropped again within a few weeks when the USA threatened to break off diplomatic relations. At this point Tirpitz resigned. Such inconsistency was indicative of the divisions and uncertainties within the German politico-military leadership about how the war could be successfully prosecuted.

The limitations of German strategic thinking were revealed further in 1916. Falkenhayn believed that the war could only be won on the western front and to this end his plan to launch a massive assault against

Gott strafe England - *God punish England*

the key French fortress of Verdun in order to drag the French into a war
of attrition was accepted. The war of attrition duly took place, but the
casualties were horrifying and the French in the end held on. The failure
at Verdun along with the losses suffered in the Battle of the Somme
undermined Falkenhayn's position completely and he was replaced in
the summer of 1916 by the joint leadership of Hindenburg and
Ludendorff.

In the years 1915-16 Germany had been unable to break the deadlock
created by the failure of the Schlieffen Plan. Alternative strategies either
lacked imagination or were pursued without real commitment. As one
historian has put it: 'What they [the Germans] could not do was escape
from the remorseless logic of a two-front war'. And as victory failed to
materialise the economic pressures of conflict grew more intense.

c) The Limitations of German Economic Mobilisation

Germany's economic growth was the foundation stone of its emergence
as a world power in the years before 1914 (see page 10). Such economic
strength was in turn dependent above all on Germany's ability to trade.
However, the imposition of the blockade and the demands of a long
drawn out conflict created enormous economic strains. Germany's
banks and export industries were badly disrupted, whilst Germany's
ability to import foodstuffs and raw materials was severely curtailed.
Some items, such as oil, rubber, nitrates and the metals copper and

mercury, were vital to war production. Others, such as fats and fertilizers were essential if Germany's population was to be adequately fed. Of course, Germany was not alone in experiencing such problems, but her circumstances meant that the situation was more marked, and, therefore, success in the war necessitated the total mobilisation of the nation's economy.

The urgency of the situation was soon recognised in some quarters. Walther Rathenau, the owner of Germany's largest electricity company, was instrumental in the creation of the KRA, *Kriegsrohstoffabteilung* (War Raw Materials Department), within the War Ministry. The KRA oversaw a range of companies whose function it was to acquire, store and distribute the most vital raw materials in the interest of the war effort. Such direct government intervention was most clearly shown over the shortage of nitrates, which were central to the manufacture of explosives. The KRA not only established a chemicals section, but also backed the construction of several plants to produce nitrates by the artificial process of nitrogen fixation. Within six months the KRA had successfully organised the provision of most essential supplies and forestalled the looming munitions crisis.

State intervention became increasingly apparent in other fields as well. Labour was affected by the role of the War Ministry in deciding who should be conscripted and who exempted, and the need to preserve industrial peace saw the creation of local War Boards made up of

In Deo Gratia *by Böhl*

representatives of management and labour. There were also attempts to
regulate consumption by means of rationing and price controls: bread
rationing was introduced in early 1915 and by the end of 1916 it had
been extended to all foodstuffs (though, as will be shown in the next
section, such measures did not allay social discontent).

In the short-term the measures taken by the German leadership to
regulate the war economy were reasonably successful. However, military
victory was not forthcoming in 1915-16 and thus two crucial economic
weaknesses continued to erode Germany's capacity to maintain the fight
in the long-term; these were the government budget and the provision of
food. Germany was already running a massive government deficit in
peace-time and once the war started it soared. The issue of war bonds
represented the only real attempt to narrow the gap between income and
expenditure. The idea of raising taxes on income and industrial profits,
the burden of which would have fallen more on the rich, was rejected on
political grounds. The cost of the war was simply put off until
reparations could be extracted from the defeated. Altogether only 16 per
cent of the cost of the war was met from taxation. Such a massive
expansion of the money supply not only fuelled inflation, but also
eroded the value of the mark. Even more disturbing was Germany's
inability to feed itself. The effects of the blockade and the conscription of
so many able-bodied males led to a marked decline in grain production
and yet attempts to establish government control over the agricultural
economy met only with resistance from the powerful lobby of
landowners. Eventually, a War Nutrition Office was set up in 1916 to
regulate food supplies, but its measures proved inadequate. Production
continued to decline and because insufficient food was made available at
the regulated prices the black market flourished even more.

By the end of 1916 the economic exigencies of the situation were such
that the OHL determined to intensify the war effort by a clearly defined
set of targets. The Hindenburg Programme aimed to increase arms
production massively by placing contracts directly with heavy industry,
whilst the introduction of the Auxiliary Service Law was supposed to
achieve 'the mobilisation of the entire civilian population for war
service'. In fact, both initiatives fell short of their objectives and
problems of labour and production continued to dog the German war
effort.

The onset of 'total war' induced Germany to use the power of the
state as a means of mobilising its economic potential. However, there
were distinct limits on how far this policy could go because of certain key
interest groups. Ironically, therefore, autocratic Germany failed to
achieve the same degree of mobilisation as in democratic Britain where
war-time consensus and collectivism proved to be more productive in
the long run. In Germany the First World War did not result in a state
controlled economy: government fiscal policy was unchanged; industries were not nationalised; and the property rights of landowners were

left relatively untouched. In this sense the German economy was never fully mobilised to meet the military necessities of the situation. And yet, as will be seen in the next section, the consequences of this economic policy were to be disastrous in the long-term for the stability of the *Kaiserreich,* since the political blame for the nation's problems was increasingly placed at the door of the state.

d) Submarine Warfare and the Entry of the USA

Although Hindenburg and Ludendorff were determined to pursue the war with the utmost vigour and to reject any possibility of a compromise peace, they were unable to offer any fundamentally new military strategy. There was no way out of the deadlock on the western front and yet the passage of time simply played further into the hands of the Allies. It was this dilemma which encouraged the OHL to press once again for the implementation of unrestricted submarine warfare in the self-deluding belief that this would bring Britain to its knees. Bethmann remained unconvinced by this 'miracle cure' and its possible side-effects, but by January 1917 he was politically too isolated to offer effective resistance and the following month a new submarine campaign was launched. Within a few months the bankruptcy of the policy was only too apparent. Admittedly, Britain had initially suffered catastrophic losses, but the introduction of the convoy system proved decisive in reducing the losses to tolerable levels in the latter half of 1917 and by 1918 it was clear that the Germans were losing the submarine war. Even more significantly, the USA declared war in April 1917. Military logistics were now stacked against Germany. The resources of the world's greatest economic power - finance, industry, and manpower - were mobilised in the interests of the Allies, whilst the economic strains on Germany and the Central Powers continued to increase.

e) The Collapse of Germany's Final Offensive

Germany's defeat seemed only a matter of time as 1917 drew to a close. The fact that Germany did not actually succumb until November 1918 was mainly due to events in Russia, where the establishment of the Bolshevik regime in November 1917 resulted in an armistice with Germany and then a negotiated peace in March 1918 (the Treaty of Brest-Litovsk - see page 71). This provided a window of opportunity for the German leadership. Not only did it boost civilian and military morale at a critical time, but it also liberated Germany from the nightmare of the two-front war and opened up the chance to snatch victory by concentrating German military might on the western front.

However, although Germany's victory offensive in the west, 'Operation Michael', at first made considerable progress and German troops once again crossed the Marne in June, the Allied lines were never decisively broken and the offensive slowly ground to a halt. There were several reasons for this. Ironically, the OHL had still kept one and a half million men on the eastern front to establish and maintain control over Germany's newly won sphere of influence - such numbers could have provided vital reserves to maintain the momentum of advance. Instead, German troops in the west were confronted by ever increasing numbers of American troops, who had not been subjected to the debilitating effects of trench warfare for the past three years. When the Allies counter-attacked in August German troops proved incapable of withstanding the assault, although their retreat remained an orderly one. By mid-September the western states of Germany faced the very real possibility of invasion, whilst in the south-east of Europe Germany's allies, Turkey, Bulgaria, and Austria-Hungary all faced imminent collapse. Even Hindenburg and Ludendorff at last recognised the extent of the crisis and on 29 September they advised the emperor that Germany must sue for an armistice - the war had been lost.

f) Conclusion

With hindsight there appears to have been almost an inevitability about Germany's defeat in the First World War once the Schlieffen Plan failed to achieve the rapid victory which the German military leadership recognised as so vital. And yet, although logic suggested that a two-front war could not be won by Germany, it proved politically impossible to accept a compromise peace. Thus, the war developed a momentum of its own. The surrender of Russia in early 1918 did briefly offer the possibility of an escape from 'the strategic strait-jacket', but by that time German capacity to mobilise and maintain a major offensive, particularly in the face of the American entry into the war and the collapse of its own allies, was insufficient to affect the outcome.

2 The Domestic Impact of War

a) *Burgfriede*

Essentially, Germany went to war in August 1914 united in a patriotic fervour against what was perceived as the threat posed by 'barbaric Russia'. The mood of the moment was caught by numerous writers, who saw the war as a mixture of adventure and liberation. Bruno Frank's contemporary poem was typical:

Proud Times, 1914

Rejoice, friends, that we are alive
And that we're young and nimble!
Never was there a year like this,

And never such a gift for youth!
It is given to us to take our stand or to strike out
Eastwards or westwards.
The greatest of all of earth's ages
Sets its brand upon our young hearts.

The consensus was reflected at a political level as well. A political truce, *Burgfriede,* was agreed by all parties and the necessary war-credits to finance the war were passed unanimously. Even the Social Democrats, who for so long had been viewed as unpatriotic pacifist 'enemies of the state' promised their support for a 'defensive war'. Their attitude came as a surprise to many in the military who had been seriously considering the need to make mass arrests and to impose press censorship as a way of keeping them in check. However, such methods were not required for several reasons: firstly, the party was taken in by the way the government successfully managed to portray the war as a 'defensive war' against what many socialists considered a most repressive and reactionary regime. Secondly, many ordinary Social Democrats were actually very patriotic and genuinely proud of their country's achievements. This in turn contributed to a belief - particularly amongst the more moderate elements of the leadership - that by showing loyalty in the nation's hour of crisis the party could gain political legitimacy which in the long run would enhance the possibility of genuine democratisation.

The failure to secure a quick victory and the onset of military stalemate by Christmas 1914 certainly did much to undermine the enthusiastic 'spirit of August 1914'. However, dissident views remained few in number during the first half of the war. Lulled into a false sense of security by the power of the military censors and official propaganda, the public mood remained confident of eventual victory until the losses of Verdun and the Somme eventually began to tell their own story. The *Burgfriede* had lasted well over two years during which time the government had faced no real opposition from the public or the *Reichstag.* The debates, ironically, were limited to the ranks of the politico-military leadership, where individuals and factions jockeyed to exert the dominant political strategic influence.

b) The 'Silent Dictatorship'

It has already been seen how Germany's military leaders were able to justify intervention in the economy on the grounds of military necessity and how the administrative bodies were established under the control of the War Ministry. Such developments were to a large extent quite understandable. However, as the war progressed the OHL was increasingly able to interfere in political affairs with only a limited degree of political accountability. Why was this?

Firstly, there was the position of the Kaiser himself. Whatever controversies may exist about the Kaiser's political influence in the pre-war years, there is little doubt that he exerted no real control over political and military affairs during the war. His self-confidence and determination, already badly shaken by the *Daily Telegraph* affair, seemed to desert him with the onset of war and all its accompanying problems. Despite being supreme war-lord he was kept in the dark about military developments and his advice was rarely sought. As a political leader he was no more than a figure-head and an increasingly distant one at that. He did not even make a serious attempt to project a propaganda image of himself as the caring leader of his people, preferring instead to while away his time on his estates. However, the impotence of the Kaiser also had important repercussions for the power exerted by the chancellor. Bethmann did not enjoy popular backing and the *Burgfriede* in the *Reichstag* was pursued because of patriotic loyalty, not out of deference to the chancellor. All along, Bethmann's power base had been the support of the Kaiser and yet as the war progressed that support became increasingly unreliable. This left Bethmann and his government increasingly isolated and incapable of resisting the encroachments of the military.

In the summer of 1916 the developing political crisis came to a head. By this time, of course, the military situation was a cause of grave concern and many conservatives looked to place the blame on Bethmann himself. The policy of unrestricted submarine warfare had already generated divisions between the government and military and Bethmann's abandonment of the policy for the second time was viewed with suspicion. Another cause of conservative resentment was Bethmann's conciliatory approaches to the SPD, which he felt were necessary in order to maintain a political consensus in support of the war. This culminated in Bethmann successfully persuading the Kaiser to accept the need to reform Prussia's outdated franchise system. This, in turn, made him conscious of the need to shore up his own political position by winning popular support. He therefore decided to ditch Falkenhayn and to replace him with the popular military hero Hindenburg, who had so successfully led the German forces on the eastern front. On 29 August 1916 Hindenburg and his deputy Ludendorff were given joint command of the OHL.

The emergence of Hindenburg and Ludendorff was indeed a watershed, but not in the way intended by Bethmann. Far from strengthening his position, Bethmann soon found that his and the emperor's authority had been decisively weakened, since neither of them enjoyed the degree of popular backing of Hindenburg and Ludendorff. Thus, by the simple expedient of threatening resignation the OHL was able to exert an increasingly powerful influence over events, both political and economic as well as military. With the authority of the emperor and the chancellor so greatly weakened, the two main props of the Bismarckian constitution had been decisively undermined. To all intents and purposes effective power for the next two years lay with 'the silent dictatorship' of the OHL. Several opportunities for a compromise peace were quickly vetoed; ministers were replaced and promoted at its behest; and the Auxiliary Service Law was introduced to militarise society (see page 62). Eventually, the OHL forced the hapless Bethmann out of office in July 1917. He had once again opposed the reintroduction of unrestricted submarine warfare in February; he had raised the possibility of constitutional reform by establishing in March a special parliamentary committee to consider the issue; and in July he had been unable to prevent the passage of the *Reichstag* peace resolution (see page 70). Wilhelm was unwilling to let his chancellor go, but he recognised where the real power now lay. Bethmann resigned and was succeeded by the virtually unknown Michaelis - 'the fairy angel tied to the Christmas tree at Christmas for the children's benefit', as one SPD deputy described him.

In the last year of the war the power of the OHL reached new heights. The constitutional authority of the emperor and the chancellor were effectively sidelined. Even the *Reichstag*, having expressed its will for peace, proved unable or unwilling to exert any further political pressure. Instead, the latent power of the army which, had been such a key feature of the *Kaiserreich* ever since its foundation, had, under the conditions of total war eventually become overt. The real masters of Germany were the 'silent dictators', Hindenburg and Ludendorff.

c) The Human Experience

The First World War was unlike any other previous conflict for the combatants and it is impossible to convey in a few words the real horrors of that warfare. Its impact upon millions of Germans was profound in the extreme. Germany's war dead totalled 2.4 millions - 16 per cent of those conscripted. Millions more suffered permanent disabilities, both physical and mental. Such statistics of course fail to convey the human and emotional consequences. Few families escaped the trauma of a death or a casualty - and in that sense the experience of war was almost, but not quite, all-pervasive. By 1918 a popular joke was circulating on the lines of: 'What family is going to survive the war with all six sons alive?'. It was a bitter comment not only on Germany's human tragedy, but also on the declining popularity of the Hohenzollern dynasty.

Any assessment of the results of such war experiences is fraught with difficulty. It is easy to generalise and it would be easy to be wrong. Perhaps, the safe conclusion is the most accurate one - different people were affected in very different ways. Some soldiers in the trenches were drawn to left-wing politics in the hope of creating a socialist society without war. Others, like Hitler, found the discipline, selflessness and camaraderie of the trenches fulfilling and so turned war, nationalism and death into heroic ideals which they wished to transpose to post-war

German society. Many more simply grew resentful of the sacrifices made whilst rumours circulated about the luxury and indulgence to be found behind the lines amongst the higher ranking officers. Within the ranks of the navy things were very different since the lack of military activity was the cause of boredom and frustration. However, it should be noted that despite the signs of disaffection and resentment within the German military machine, there was no large scale break-down of discipline and order until the last few weeks of the war. Only when the war was lost and political change had begun did the discontent within the military combine with the growing unrest within the civilian population.

Indices of real wages 1913-19

Year	Railwaymen	Printers	Miners	Civil Servants
1913	100.0	100.0	100.0	100.0
1914	97.2	97.2	93.3	97.2
1915	79.7	77.3	81.3	77.3
1916	69.2	60.6	74.4	58.9
1917	63.9	49.4	62.7	48.6
1918	83.9	54.1	63.7	55.0
1919	92.2	72.3	82.4	54.8

Strikes and lock-outs 1913-19

Year	No. of strikes	No. of workers	Working days lost
1913	2464	0.323m	11.76m
1915	141	0.015m	0.04m
1917	562	0.668m	1.86m
1919	3719	2.132m	33.08m

On the home front the impact of war slowly, but remorselessly, impinged itself upon the lives of ordinary Germans. For the first two years the effects were generally those of inconvenience rather than real hardship, but the accumulation of shortages, the effects of inflation and the black market, and the bleak military situation began to affect the public mood by the autumn of 1916. Undoubtedly, the situation was worse in the towns than in the countryside, since farmers inevitably looked after their own interests first. But for the urban masses living standards were declining. Only those workers involved in the essential war industries were able to exploit their strong bargaining position and thereby avoid the material problems facing the rest. In the so-called 'turnip winter' of 1916-17 the situation deteriorated sharply. An exceptionally cold winter combined with a poor potato crop contributed to a disastrous food and fuel crisis. The following summer the cereal harvest fell to half that of 1913 - and yet many workers were being forced to work even longer hours as a result of the Auxiliary Service Law. Civilian deaths from starvation and hypothermia increased from 121,000 in 1916 to 293,000 in 1918, whilst infant mortality increased by over 50 per cent in the course of the war years.

In fact, 'the emergency of total war failed to create a genuine inter-class solidarity, but furthered group egotism' (Berghahn) with the result that social discontent grew markedly. Considerable anger was harboured against the 'sharks' of industry who had made vast profits from the war. Resentment grew in the minds of many within the middle class who saw their status as well as their income declining. Above all, opposition began to grow against a political leadership which urged total war, but seemed incapable of guaranteeing equality of sacrifice. Such social polarisation was further reflected in the heated political debate over Germany's war aims.

d) War Aims

The issue of war aims was central to the political and socio-economic changes taking place in war time Germany, since it went beyond a debate over simple territorial acquisitions. It also directly concerned the fundamental question of what kind of Germany was to prevail after the war. For this reason Bethmann was keen to avoid a public debate on war aims. He saw the maintenance of the *Burgfriede* as essential and he feared that discussion of war aims would be both divisive at home and detrimental to Germany's status, especially among neutral powers, abroad.

Bethmann's dilemma was that once the military stalemate had set in by 1915 two very different versions of the future peace began to emerge inside Germany. There were those who believed that Germany was fighting a purely defensive war, not one of conquest. This aspiration was most clearly felt within the ranks of the SPD, which upheld that the peace should be based upon compromise, reconciliation and no annexations. On the other hand there were those who argued for a *Siegfriede*, a peace of victory, by which Germany would exploit its position of strength to create a politico-economic hegemony over the continent and thus finally achieve its long-cherished world-power status. This objective found expression in its most extreme form in the programme of the Pan-German League which stood for the creation of a Central African empire, the annexation of key military and industrial regions in the Low Countries and northern France, the economic subjugation of western Europe to German interests, and the annexation of extensive territories in the east from Russia. Moreover, such ideas were not limited to a lunatic fringe of the ultra-conservative right-wing - the basic concept of the *Siegfriede* with some variations had a broad spectrum of political and social support. All the main parties (except the SPD) supported some version of annexationist peace and this in turn reflected the growth in influence of such views amongst broad sections of the middle class as well as the upper class. However, this was not just blind expansionist nationalism - it was an outgrowth of the fear that unless Germany achieved a decisive victory with territorial acquisitions and monetary compensation from the defeated it would prove impossible to preserve the existing social and political order from radical upheaval. In this sense the pursuit of the *Siegfriede* was seen as an essential element in the maintenance of the domestic status quo - whilst a reconciliation peace was directly associated with internal reform.

The emergence of this dichotomy in the course of 1915 had all manner of implications for a chancellor who desired to maintain a united political front in the *Reichstag* and in the nation at large. His own personal sympathies were undoubtedly with some kind of *Siegfriede* - though historians disagree about how close he came to a Pan-German view - but he was astute enough to recognise the dangers of expressing this openly. For this reason Bethmann's oft-quoted September Programme of 1914, which outlined specific German annexations in the west, the desirability of ending Russian influence on Germany's eastern frontier and finally the need to create a German-dominated European economic association, always remained a secret memorandum. It was never official government policy. Bethmann worked hard to avoid the developing polarisation, but the worsening social and military situation from the middle of 1916 only served to increase the agitation and accentuate the divisions over war aims. In 1917 his middle of the road stance proved to be no longer tenable as the pressure increased from both the left and the right. The growing political interference of the OHL totally undermined his tentative overture of peace to Russia and the USA. In April 1917 he felt obliged to endorse the Kreuznach Programme of the OHL - an extravagant list of war aims, including outright annexations in both east and west and the extension of German economic rights. Although Bethmann claimed that this document would not stand in his way if a genuine chance of a negotiated peace emerged, it was clear that his room for manoeuvre was running out. His 'support' for Kreuznach inevitably reduced further his credibility with the non-conservative forces. The political situation was further radicalised by the revolutionary overthrow of the Tsar in Russia and the split in the SPD, which saw the emergence of an Independent Social Democratic Party (USPD) wholly committed to a speedy end to the war. Thus, when Erzberger, the radical voice of the Centre, and previously an ardent annexationist proposed in July 1917 a peace resolution there emerged a coalition of forces in the *Reichstag* to support a motion which stated: 'The *Reichstag* strives for a peace of understanding and permanent reconciliation of peoples. Forced territorial acquisitions and political, economic and financial oppressions are irrecon-

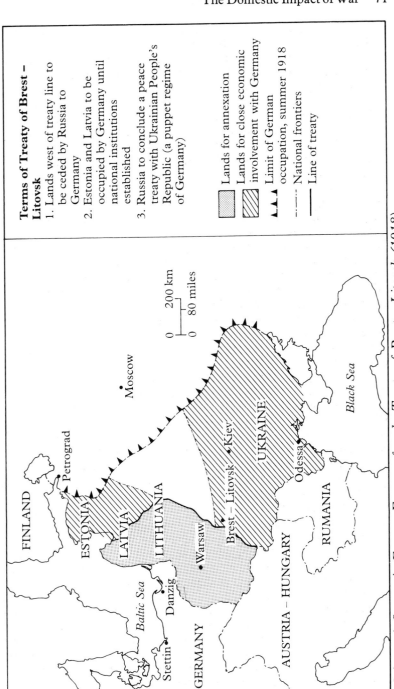

Terms of Treaty of Brest – Litovsk

1. Lands west of treaty line to be ceded by Russia to Germany
2. Estonia and Latvia to be occupied by Germany until national institutions established
3. Russia to conclude a peace treaty with Ukrainian People's Republic (a puppet regime of Germany)

Lands for annexation

Lands for close economic involvement with Germany

▲▲▲ Limit of German occupation, summer 1918

--- National frontiers

— Line of treaty

German influence in Eastern Europe after the Treaty of Brest – Litovsk (1918) cilable with such a peace'. The peace resolution was passed by 212 votes to 126.

Although Bethmann resigned, nothing was really achieved by the peace resolution. The *Reichstag* did not seize the opportunity to assert its own claims to political authority or to demand negotiations for peace. Equally, the OHL did not change its policy. Indeed, the appointment of the compliant Michaelis as chancellor merely served to strengthen further the political hold of Hindenburg and Ludendorff, who rejected out of hand anything less than the Kreuznach Programme. To this end the OHL was instrumental a few months later in the creation of the *Vaterlandspartei*, the Fatherland Party, which deliberately set out to mobilise mass support behind the OHL by giving political expression to the demands of the extreme right wing. Led by Tirpitz and financially backed by some of the leading pressure groups from industry, it proved remarkably successful and by 1918 it boasted 1.2 million members.

The creation of the *Vaterlandspartei* and the passage of the peace resolution are indicative of how Germany had become divided into two increasingly hostile camps. Those who called for a compromise peace without forced annexations were essentially the supporters of constitutional reform: those who backed the Fatherland Party were equally likely to uphold the political status quo.

At the beginning of 1918 it seemed as if the forces of conservatism would emerge supreme. The Treaty of Brest-Litovsk represented a decisive victory for the supporters of *Siegfriede*. A *Siegfriede* on this scale not only liberated Germany from the two-front war and made victory in the west feasible, but also massively strengthened the political standing of the military leadership. The *Reichstag*, for example, backed the treaty by a large majority - only the USPD voted against it. However, there were already widespread strikes in Germany's major cities in early 1918. The OHL remained oblivious to the implications of the socio-economic foment and placed a blind faith in victory in the west and the imposition of another *Siegfriede*. Thus, when the hoped-for military victory did not materialise, a revolutionary situation emerged. F. Meinecke in a letter to a friend, 21 October 1918 remarked:

1 A fearful and gloomy existence awaits us in the best of circumstances! And although my hatred of the enemy, who remind me of beasts of prey, is as hot as ever, so is my anger and resentment at those German power politicians who, by their
5 presumption and their stupidity, have dragged us down into this abyss. Repeatedly in the course of the war, we could have had a peace by agreement, if it had not been that boundless demands of the Pan-German-militaristic-conservative combine made it impossible. It is fearful and tragic that this combine could be broken only
10 by the overthrow of the whole state.

e) Conclusion

The importance of the First World War in shaping Germany's historical development cannot be over-emphasised. A German military victory in 1918 would almost certainly have defused the crisis and in so doing retarded the process of political reform for a generation or more. Instead, four years of total war culminating in defeat brought the *Kaiserreich* to its knees. It massively dislocated the economy, wrecking the already parlous government finances which in turn initiated run-away monetary inflation. It was the cause of serious social tensions which accentuated class differences. And it exacerbated the polarisation of politics of the *Kaiserreich*. In pre-war Germany there had been constitutional instability and occasional political crises. By the autumn of 1918, however, Germany found itself in a revolutionary situation.

3 The German Revolution 1918-19

a) October Reform - a Revolution from Above?

By late September 1918 the military defeat of Germany was a certainty - even Ludendorff recognised the fact. Faced with the prospect of an Allied invasion of German territory and the possibility of radical internal disturbances, Ludendorff sanctioned, with the Kaiser's consent, the conversion of Germany into a constitutional monarchy. Ludendorff's volte-face was primarily motivated by a two-fold desire: to pre-empt social revolution from the populace at large, and to secure for Germany the best possible peace settlement from the Allies, who, it was believed, were likely to be more sympathetic to a democratic regime in Berlin. Yet, even at this stage a third and far more cynical motive was already apparent - the need to remove responsibility for Germany's defeat away from the military and conservative establishment and instead to transfer blame on to appropriate 'scapegoats'. Here are the origins of the 'Stab-in the-Back' myth, which was to play such a vital part in the history of the Weimar Republic (see page 100). It was a theme soon recognised by others. The Bavarian military attaché reported in October:

1 On the domestic political situation one often hears the opinion expressed that it is a good thing that the left-wing parties will have to incur the odium for peace. The storm of indignation of the people will fall on them ... One hopes that then one can get back
5 into the saddle and continue to govern according to the old recipe.

It was in this context that Prince Max von Baden, a moderate conservative, became chancellor of a government on 3 October which included representatives from the SPD and the Left Liberals. In the following month a series of constitutional reforms came into effect which made Germany into a parliamentary democracy: the three-class franchise was abolished in Prussia; the emperor conceded his powers over the army and the navy to the *Reichstag;* and the chancellor and the government were made accountable to the *Reichstag* not instead of the Kaiser. At the same time armistice negotiations with the Allies were initiated.

Taken together these changes have traditionally been portrayed as 'a revolution from above'. Such an interpretation has not been questioned by structuralist historians, who see the events of October 1918 as exemplifying their manipulation theory of control by the elites. Wehler writes: 'The conservative bastions of the monarchy and the army were to be preserved as far as possible behind the facade of new arrangements intended to prevent the radical overthrow of the system and prove acceptable to the Allies'. However, more recently it has been suggested by some historians, such as Kolb, that the initiative of the OHL coincided with increasing pressure from the *Reichstag* to bring about political change. The most telling evidence in support of this interpretation is the resolution passed (on the same day as Ludendorff's recommendation for an armistice) demanding 'the creation of a strong government supported by the confidence of a majority of the *Reichstag*'. Furthermore, Prince Max was appointed only after consultation with the majority parties in the *Reichstag.*

The idea of a *Reichstag* initiative certainly cannot be ignored but on balance it would be wrong to read too much into its actions. Over the years the *Reichstag* had shown no real inclination to seize the constitutional initiative. When opportunities like the *Daily Telegraph* affair, the Zabern Affair and the peace resolution had arisen, it had made no real attempt to press home its advantage. Likewise, in 1918. The *Reichstag* adjourned on 5 October and went into recess until 22 October, when it adjourned again until 9 November. These were hardly the actions of an institution that wished to shape events decisively. The October reforms were essentially imposed from above and the *Reichstag* was happy to acquiesce. However, it would be an exaggeration to see these fundamental constitutional changes as representing a revolution. The social and economic forces which had dominated imperial Germany were still entrenched at the end of the month. What pushed Germany in such a short space of time from mere political reform towards revolution was the public realisation that the war was indeed lost. The shock of defeat, after years of hardship and optimistic propaganda, significantly radicalised popular attitudes. By early November it was apparent that a constitutional monarchy, with Wilhelm II as sovereign and a prince as chancellor, could not defuse a truly revolutionary situation.

b) The Birth of the Republic - the November Revolution

There can be little doubt that a genuinely revolutionary situation

prevailed in Germany in early November 1918. What is more debatable
is the nature of the revolutionary feeling. What were the political
alternatives facing Germany at this time, and why did the so-called
November Revolution result in the creation of the Weimar Republic as
opposed to any other system?

Prince Max's government began to lose control of the political
situation as a result of a sailors' revolt at Kiel, which had been prompted
by a real fear that their officers were intent on a suicide sortie to redeem
the honour of the navy. The news of the Kiel mutiny fanned the flames
of discontent throughout Germany and by 8 November numerous
workers' and soldiers' councils had been established in the major cities.
In Munich the Wittelsbach dynasty was deposed and an independent
democratic socialist republic was proclaimed. Such a spontaneous wave
of popular discontent suggests that the October reforms had failed to
impress, and that a revolutionary momentum had developed, whose
minimum requirements were immediate peace and the abdication of the
Kaiser.

Of course, the revolutionary wave which swept Germany was not a
united force. There were essentially three strands to the revolutionary
movement. The SPD, led by Ebert and Scheidemann, represented
moderate reformist socialism. Above all, the party upheld democracy
and constitutionalism and it rejected unequivocally anything that might
have been equated with Soviet-style communism. An editorial in its
newspaper on 24 December 1918 stated:

1 It was hunger that forced the Russian people under the yoke of
militarism. Russia's workers went on strike, destroyed the
economy through over-hasty socialisation, deprived themselves of
the means of making a living through unrealisable demands, and
5 sacrificed their freedom to militarism. Bolshevik militarism is the
violent despotism of a clique ...

Let the Russian example be a warning. Do we want another
war? Do we want terror, the bloody reign of a caste? NO! We want
no more bloodshed and no militarism. We want to achieve peace
10 through work. We want peace, in order not to degenerate into a
militarism dictated by the unemployed, as in Russia. Bolshevik
bums call the armed masses into the streets, and armed masses,
bent on violence, are militarism personified. But we do not want
militarism of the right or of the left.
15   Bolshevism, the lazy man's militarism, knows no freedom or
equality. It is vandalism and terror by a small group that arrogates
power. So do not follow Spartacus, the German Bolsheviks, unless
you want to ruin our economy and trade.

On the extreme left stood the Spartakists, led by Rosa Luxemburg (one
of the few women to be prominent in German political history) and Karl

Liebknecht. Intoxicated by events in Russia, they believed that Germany should follow a similar road. They campaigned for a socialist republic, based on the people's power in the workers' and soldiers' councils, which would abolish the institutions of imperial Germany. To these ends they spurned the SDP's 'bourgeois' compromises and took to the streets, organising demonstrations, strikes, and eventually an armed insurrection!. The Spartakist manifesto of 1918 stated:

1 The question today is not democracy or dictatorship. The question that history has put on the agenda reads: *bourgeois* democracy or *socialist* democracy. For the dictatorship of the proletariat is democracy in the socialist sense of the word. Dictatorship of the
5 proletariat does not mean bombs, putsches, riots and anarchy, as the agents of capitalist profits deliberately and falsely claim. Rather, it means using all instruments of political power to achieve socialism, to expropriate the capitalist class, through and in accordance with the will of the revolutionary majority of the
10 proletariat.

Caught between the two extremes of the revolution was the USPD. It demanded radical social and economic change to complement the political reforms, fearing that otherwise democracy would not survive. However, as a political movement it was far from united and its actual influence was seriously curtailed by factional squabbles, particularly between those who sympathised with the creation of a parliamentary democracy and those who advocated a more revolutionary democracy based on the workers' councils. The wide range of differing aims and methods amongst the revolutionaries is a partial explanation of why the events of November 1918 are so very confusing for the history student. However, it should be remembered that reality was far from clear to many contemporary political figures, who were trying to make decisions in a society which to all intents and purposes was in a state of collapse.

Prince Max would certainly have liked to preserve the institution of the monarchy, if not Wilhelm II himself, but the emperor's delusions that he could carry on placed the chancellor in an invidious position. In the end, Prince Max became so worried that the revolutionary situation in Berlin might be getting out of hand that on 9 November he announced the formation under Ebert of a new SPD/USPD coalition government which proclaimed a republic. It was only at this point that the Kaiser, prompted by leading generals, accepted the reality of the situation and went into voluntary exile in Holland.

Ebert's main worry was that in this situation the extreme left would gain the upper hand. He saw the growing number of workers' councils as comparable to Russian-style soviets which threatened his chosen path of evolution and legitimacy. He was determined to prevent the descent into civil strife by maintaining law and order and he feared that the return of millions of troops after the armistice agreement, which was eventually signed on 11 November, would create enormous social and political problems. These were the crucial concerns in the minds of Ebert and the SPD leadership in the months that followed. On 10 November General Groener, Ludendorff's successor, telephoned Ebert. The OHL agreed to support the government and to maintain law and order, in return for a promise from Ebert to resist Bolshevism and to preserve the authority of the officers. The Ebert-Groener Pact was followed a few days later by the Stinnes-Legien Agreement between the employers and the trade unions. In return for a commitment not to interfere with private ownership and the free market, the unions were guaranteed full legal recognition, workers' committees and the eight-hour working day. These two agreements have been severely criticised, particularly by the left wing, as compromises with the forces of conservatism, but for Ebert and the SPD they not only acted as guarantees of stability and peaceful transition, but also strengthened the government's hand against the extreme left.

By early 1919 it was clear that the SPD had become distanced from the USPD, its previous allies on the left. On 1 January 1919 the Spartakists formally founded the *Kommunistische Partei Deutschlands* (KPD - German Communist Party). It refused to participate in the parliamentary elections, preferring instead to place its faith in the workers' councils. Meanwhile the USPD members of Ebert's government had resigned over the shooting of some Spartakists by soldiers. The SPD government was increasingly isolated. It therefore drifted further to the right and grew dependent on the civil service and the army to maintain effective government. The reality of the changing power balance was revealed when the Spartakists attempted to overthrow the government in January 1919 by an armed uprising. They had little chance of success. The government used army troops, but also 'irregular' paramilitary groups, *Freikorps* - right-wing nationalist ex-soldiers, who were only too willing to suppress communist activity.

The Spartakist coup was defeated relatively easily with Liebknecht and Luxemburg being brutally murdered whilst in police custody. This event set the tone for the next few months. The elections for the National Assembly duly took place, though the continuation of strikes and street disorders in Berlin resulted in the Assembly's first meeting being switched to the town of Weimar. More serious disturbances in Bavaria in April resulted in a short-lived soviet republic being established there. Both episodes were effectively brought under control by the *Freikorps,* though in each case at the cost of several hundred lives. The infant republic had successfully survived the traumas of its birth.

For many years historians assumed that there had only ever been two possible options available to Germany at the end of the war: a communist dictatorship or a parliamentary republic in the style of Weimar. In this way Ebert was portrayed as a near heroic figure whose pragmatism had saved Germany from Bolshevism. In the wake of extensive research in the 1960s such a simplified interpretation has been revised. Close analysis of the workers' councils movement throughout Germany has shown that very few fell under the control of the extreme left. The vast majority were initially led by the SPD with USPD support and only after January 1919 did the USPD come to dominate. Thus, it is now generally recognised that the threat from the communists was grossly over-estimated. They may well have been vocal in putting forward their revolutionary creed, but their actual base of support was minimal. This evidence has in turn led to a reassessment of Ebert and the SPD leadership. Although their integrity and sincerity have not been questioned, it is claimed that their reading of the political situation was poor. Blinded by their fear of the left, they exaggerated the threat from that quarter and thereby compromised with the conservative forces of imperial Germany, when in actual fact there was no need, if only they had been prepared to assert authority. In that sense they missed the opportunity to create a solidly based republic built on socialist and democratic principles.

c) Conclusion: What Revolution?

By May 1919 a degree of stability had returned to Germany. The German revolution had run its course and the Weimar Republic had

Cheers Noske! The Young Revolution is Dead *by G Grosz (1919)*

been established. However, serious doubts remain about the nature and real extent of these supposedly revolutionary changes. Indeed, some historians argue that there was no real revolution at all.

Undoubtedly, there existed the potential for a revolutionary upheaval in Germany as the war came to an end. The effects of war and the trauma of defeat shook the faith of large numbers of the populace in the old order. The *Kaiserreich* could not survive and it did not. The Kaiser and the other princes were deposed and parliamentary democracy was introduced. These were important changes. However, in the end the revolution did not go much further than the October reforms. It was strictly limited in scope. Society was left almost untouched by events for there was no attempt to reform the key institutions. The civil service, judiciary and army all remained essentially intact. Likewise, the economy. Improved working conditions were implemented, but there were no changes in the structure of big business and land ownership. Vital elements of continuity therefore prevailed. The SPD leadership hoped that structural change would follow in the wake of legitimate constitutional reform; but with hindsight it seems that the USPD demand for more radical change in the social and economic spheres may well have been the more appropriate policy for securing the establishment of democracy in the long-term. As it was, the divisions on the left played into the hands of the forces of conservatism and as a result 'it is more accurate to talk of a potential revolution which ran away into the sand rather than the genuine article' (Hughes). Indeed, the increasing dependency of the moderate left on the elites of imperial Germany in the first half of 1919 strongly suggests that the forces of counter-revolution were already beginning to assert a dominant influence once again.

Making notes on 'Germany in War and Revolution'

This chapter is like a lynch-pin for it serves as a link between Imperial and Weimar Germany. Therefore you have two aims. Firstly, you must try to understand why the First World War ended in the collapse of imperial Germany. But you will then also have to put this understanding into the context provided by the previous two chapters, so you are clear in your own mind as to whether the First World War was the cause or merely the occasion of the demise of the *Kaiserreich*. Secondly, you must begin to understand the difficulties of Weimar's creation, so that you are in a good position to appreciate the problems after 1919, which are covered in Chapters 5 to 7.

Following the reading of this chapter there are two important tasks to carry out:
1. Construct a chronological table for the period 1914-19. Divide your sheet of paper into three columns with the following headings:

a) Foreign/military events
   b) Domestic social/economic developments
   c) Domestic political events.
   It would be a good idea to refer to the Chronological Table on pages
   156-8 to assist you with this task.
2. You need to begin to grapple with some of the important issues of
   analysis arising from Germany's involvement in the First World
   War. Therefore, in addition to writing notes on each section, write
   brief answers to the questions that accompany the headings below.
   (i) The Causes of Germany's Defeat
   Place the five main causes in rank order and explain your reasoning.
   (ii) The Domestic Impact
   What conclusions can be drawn about the state of Imperial
   Germany from the way it managed the First World War?
   (iii) The German Revolution
   Why did the reforms of October 1918 fail to prevent the overthrow
   of the Hohenzollern monarchy one month later? Was the new
   republic decisively weakened by the circumstances of its birth?

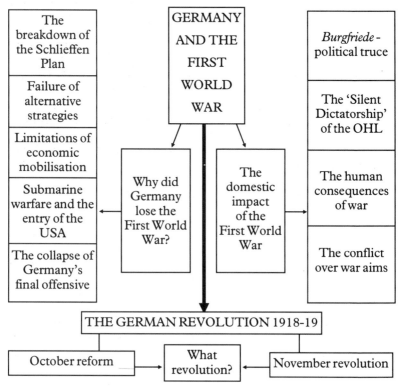

Summary - Germany in War and Revolution, 1914-19

Answering essay questions on 'Germany in War and Revolution'

Many of the essays you will be asked to write will be about historical causation. They appear in many forms but are all essentially variations on the theme of explaining the 'why' of history. Here are some examples relating to the material from this chapter:

1. Account for the failure of Germany to win the First World War.
2. Explain the collapse of Germany in 1918.
3. Why did the Ludendorff offensive of Spring 1918 collapse after initially having such success?
4. What were the reasons for the collapse of the *Kaiserreich*?
5. Why did the Kaiser abdicate in November 1918?
6. How do you explain the outbreak of revolution in Germany in Autumn 1918?

As you probably know, a good way to organise an answer to this kind of question is to draw up a series of 'because' statements, each of which could then serve as a basis for a main paragraph. But such an essay structure could still be very shapeless, unless you categorise the factors in some way. You could arrange them into logical sets such as: military, political, economic, and social factors. Alternatively, you could arrange them into long-term, medium-term and short-term factors. Try both these approaches for Question 4. Which approach do you think works more effectively?

Although both approaches would certainly form the basis for a reasonable analytical essay, you may feel that neither one is entirely satisfactory. Therefore, a more sophisticated approach would be to combine both styles within the one essay. You can see how this could be achieved, if you now complete the following table for the same question:

	Long-term	Medium-term	Short-term
Military			
Political			
Economic			
Social			

This kind of approach will not only lead to a very well-structured essay, but it will also help you to clarify in your own mind where the 'thrust' of your analysis actually lies.

Source-based questions on 'Germany in War and Revolution'

1 German Propaganda in the First World War

Carefully read Wilhelm II's proclamation on page 58 and study the two posters on pages 60-1. Answer the following questions.

a) Explain Wilhelm II's reference to 'open and secret hostility from east and west and from beyond the sea'. (2 marks)
b) Comment on the style and the content used by the Kaiser in his proclamation to justify German intervention in August 1914. (4 marks)
c) In what ways do all three sources use history itself as a tool of propaganda? (4 marks)
d) 'German propaganda in the First World War was elitist and never geared to the language of the population at large'. How far do these sources, and other evidence known to you, support this assertion? (5 marks)

2 Popular Attitudes to the War

Carefully read Frank's poem on pages 64-5 and the letter of Meinecke on page 72. Study the statistics in the table on page 68. Answer the following questions.

a) How does Frank try to convey the 'spirit of 1914'? (4 marks)
b) Write an analytical commentary based upon the statistics on pages 69. (7 marks)
c) Why was Meinecke so angry in his letter of October 1918? (3 marks)
d) What problems do these sources highlight about the assessment of public opinion at a time of war? (6 marks)

3 The German Revolution

Read carefully the report of the Bavarian military attaché (page 73), the SPD editorial (page 75) and the Spartakist manifesto (page 76). Study the painting by Grosz (page 78). Answer the following questions.

a) Explain the following references:
   (i) 'the dictatorship of the proletariat'. (2 marks).
   (ii) 'Russia's workers ... sacrificed their freedom to militarism'. (2 marks)
b) In what ways does the SPD editorial try to deride and denigrate the Spartakists? (4 marks)
c) Compare and contrast the aims of the SPD and the Spartakists. (4 marks)
d) Explain in your own words what Grosz is attempting to communicate in his painting about the German revolution. (5 marks)
e) 'The German revolution ran into the sand because of the divisions of German socialism'. To what extent do these sources substantiate this view? (8 marks)

CHAPTER 5

Weimar: the Years of Crisis, 1919-24

Despite the disturbances across Germany in the months after the collapse of the *Kaiserreich*, the new republic was able to hold its first elections for a National Assembly on 19 January 1919. Most political parties took the opportunity to re-form themselves, but new names should not disguise the fact that there was considerable continuity in the structure of the party system (see the table below). In the end, the results represented a major success for the forces of parliamentary democracy. Over three-quarters of the electorate voted for the three parties committed to the republic - the SPD, the DDP and the Centre - which then proceeded to form the first government, the so-called 'Weimar Coalition'.

However, the creation of a broadly based democratic coalition did not result in a period of stability and consolidation for the young republic. The years after 1919 were ones of almost continuous crisis and on several occasions the very survival of Weimar democracy was in doubt. Only after the critical year of 1923 was there a period of relative calm. In this chapter it will be necessary to examine the nature of the problems faced by Weimar Germany and to gauge how much of a threat they actually posed to the existence of the regime. Above all, we need to understand why Weimar was able to survive the years of crisis, whilst also assessing how serious was the destabilisation for its long-term survival.

Major Political Parties in the Weimar Republic

DDP *Deutsche Demokratische Partei.* German Democratic Party.
Formed from the old DFP or Left Liberals. Attracted support from the professional middle-classes. It upheld a curious blend of liberal and nationalist ideas.

ZP *Zentrumspartei.* Centre Party.
Initially, it tried to establish itself as the non-denominational Christian People's Party, but this was unsuccessful and it continued to be the voice of political Catholicism. Its social composition was extremely broad, ranging from aristocratic landowners to Christian trade unionists. Not all sections of the party were wholly committed to the republic.

BVP *Bayerische Volkspartei.* Bavarian People's Party.
A strong regional and Catholic party which seceded from the ZP in 1919 because of the latter's support for centralised government.

DVP   *Deutsche Volkspartei.* German People's Party.
A new party founded by Stresemann who was excluded from the DDP because of his annexationist views during the First World War. Conservative and monarchist, it was initially luke-warm towards the republic, but under Stresemann's influence it became a strong supporter of parliamentary democracy.

DNVP *Deutschenationale Volkspartei.* German National People's Party.
A right-wing party formed from the old conservative parties and some of the racist, anti-Semitic groups such as the Pan-German League. Monarchist and anti-republican. Closely tied to the interests of heavy industry and the landowners.

NSDAP *Nationalsozialistische Partei Deutschlands.* Nazi Party.
Ultra right-wing party formed in 1919. Anti-republican, anti-Semitic and strongly nationalist.

SPD   *Sozialdemokratische Partei Deutschlands.* German Social
       Democratic Party.
The moderate wing of the socialist movement. Very much the party of the working class and the trade unions. It strongly supported parliamentary democracy and was opposed to the revolutionary demands of the more left-wing socialists.

USPD   *Unabhängige Sozialdemokratische Partei Deutschlands.*
       Independent German Social Democratic Party.
The USPD broke away from the SPD in April 1917. It included many of the more revolutionary elements of German socialism and therefore sought radical social and political change. Some joined the KPD during 1919-20 whilst by 1922 most of the others had returned to the ranks of the SPD.

KPD   *Kommunistische Partei Deutschlands.* German Communist Party.
Formed in December 1918 by the extreme left-wing, e.g. Spartakists. Anti-republican in the sense that it opposed Weimar-style democracy and supported a revolutionary overthrow of society. Bolstered by the defection of many USPD members in 1920.

---

1 Two Key Documents

a) The Weimar Constitution

In view of the fact that the Weimar Republic only lasted for 14 crisis-ridden years, it is hardly surprising that its written constitution has been the focus of considerable analysis. Some historians have gone so far as to argue that in its clauses are to be found the real causes of the collapse of the republic and the success of National Socialism. The basis of such claims is rooted in three elements of the constitution: the introduction of proportional representation; the ambiguous relationship between the president and the *Reichstag*, with particular reference to the emergency powers available under Article 48; and the continuity permitted to traditional social and economic institutions.

The introduction of proportional representation became the focus of particular criticism in the two decades after 1945, when it was argued that the system had encouraged the formation of new parties and splinter parties, which in turn made it more difficult to form and to maintain governments. However, it is difficult to see how an alternative voting system based upon a British style 'first past the post' could have made for a more effective parliamentary democracy. The fundamental problem was the difficulty of creating coalitions and agreeing policies amongst the main parties - the existence of the splinter parties by comparison was a relatively minor one. As to the view that proportional representation encouraged the emergence of political extremism after 1929, it now seems clear that the changes in electoral attitudes were just too dramatic to be contained, and it may well have been the case that a system based on relative majorities would have actually facilitated the rise of Nazism and Communism.

The relationship created between the *Reichstag* and the president reflected the uncertainties felt by many of those drafting the new constitution towards the establishment of a democracy based upon parliamentary sovereignty alone. Fears of parliamentary absolutism were not only strong on the right wing, but also within liberal circles and this resulted in the creation of a presidency which was deliberately intended to act as a political counter-balance to the *Reichstag*. The president was directly elected by the people for seven years; he was supreme commander of the armed forces; he alone convened and dissolved the *Reichstag;* and he appointed the chancellor and the Reich government. The powers of the president have often been seen as amounting to those of an *Ersatzkaiser* (substitute emperor) and when set alongside the authority of the *Reichstag* it seems that the attempt to prevent a monopoly of power by one institution only succeeded in creating a dualism which was 'fundamentally ambiguous' (Sternberger). As a result a constitutional uncertainty prevailed from the start. Was the ultimate source of authority in the democratic republic vested in the representative assembly of the people or in the popularly elected head of state?

This situation was further exacerbated by the considerable powers conferred upon the president by the controversial Article 48. This key article provided the head of state with the authority to suspend civil rights in an emergency and to take whatever action was required to restore law and order by the issue of presidential decrees. The intention was to create the means by which government could continue to function in a temporary crisis. However, the effect was to create 'a constitutional anomaly' (Craig) which could allow parliamentary government to be side-lined by extra-parliamentary forces acting through the president. Of course, such fears, which were actively expressed by some deputies in the constitutional debate of 1919, assumed a particular significance during the crisis that eventually brought Hitler to power. However, it should be remembered that in the crisis of 1923 the presidential powers were used as intended and to good effect: moreover, the office of president did not in the end prove to be the means by which Hitler's dictatorship was created.

In a strange dichotomy the Weimar constitution also combined both the continuity of traditional institutions and the introduction of a wide range of progressive civil liberties. The civil service, the judiciary and the education system were all preserved (and legally enshrined) in their old form. And as the vast majority of bureaucrats, judges, and professors were luke-warm or indeed actively hostile to the republic, the result was that powerful conservative, even reactionary, forces were able to exert a high degree of influence in the daily life of the republic. Yet, this was at odds with the provision of extensive civil rights aimed at satisfying all the elements of a modern pluralistic society. In this way the spirit of the constitution was democratic and progressive, whilst the institutions remained wedded to the values of a previous era.

It is all too easy with hindsight to select those elements of the Weimar constitution which may have contributed in some part to the demise of the republic and then to highlight their significance. However, by providing an essentially liberal democratic framework the new constitution certainly represented a distinct improvement upon the authoritarian rigidity of the Bismarckian constitution and in July 1919 it was passed by a substantial and convincing majority in the *Reichstag* of 262 votes to 75. What, of course, the constitution could not control were the conditions and circumstances in which it had to operate. In this sense it is just unrealistic to imagine that any piece of paper could have made provision for all the possible consequences arising from Germany's immense problems and its divergent social and political forces. Thirty years later Theodor Heuss, the first president of the Federal Republic, addressed the founding fathers of 1949 as follows:

1 It is now fashionable ... to denigrate the Weimar Constitution. It is now customary to say that because Hitler's turn came and the provisions of the Weimar Constitution did not stop him, therefore this constitution was bad. The historical process does not work in
5 quite so primitive a manner.
    The democracy of Weimar was so slow in getting off the ground and never got properly into gear because Germany never conquered democracy for herself. Democracy came to Germany - and this has become almost banal by now - in the wake of defeat.
10 But because it was not taken by storm it could not develop its own myth nor acquire its own know-how. Thus, it happened that the

further evolution of democracy took place in an atmosphere of nationalist Romanticism and monarchical restoration and in the shadow of the wretched crime of the stab-in-the-back myth. These 15 things were much more decisive in governing the operation of the Weimar Constitution than the technical formulation of this or that constitutional paragraph, even if we may today consider some of them less than perfect.

b) The Treaty of Versailles

On 7 May 1919 the German delegation at the Paris Peace Conference was handed the draft peace treaty. Two months later, after futile attempts to negotiate concessions and after the resignation of the republic's first coalition government, the Treaty of Versailles was finally endorsed by Germany.

On no other political issue was there such universal agreement within Weimar Germany as in the rejection and condemnation of the Treaty of Versailles. The German case was based on a number of points. Firstly, the treaty was seen as a *Diktat* - a dictated settlement allowing for no negotiations and imposed under the threat of further Allied military action. Secondly, the treaty was considered to be at variance with the Fourteen Points of President Wilson, upon which Germans believed the armistice was to be based. If self-determination was indeed the guiding principle of a Wilsonian peace, Germany found it incomprehensible that Germans in Austria, Danzig, Posen and West Prussia (the Polish Corridor), Memel, Upper Silesia, the Sudetenland and the Saar were all deliberately excluded from the German state and placed under foreign rule. Likewise, the loss of German colonies and their distribution as mandates to the Allies seemed at variance with Wilson's point five for 'an impartial adjustment of all colonial claims'. Thirdly, Germany found it impossible to accept the 'war guilt' thesis which underpinned the payment of reparations. Most Germans had been convinced that the war of 1914 had been fought for defensive reasons and that in no way could Germany alone be made to accept responsibility. Consequently, the Allied argument that Germany be forced to pay extensive reparations was seen as totally unreasonable, especially when the exact sum was not actually stipulated, but was to be decided by an Allied commission at a later date. In the Germans' view this amounted to their being forced to sign a 'blank cheque'. Finally, Germany's treatment by the Allies was viewed as demeaning and unworthy of a great power. For example, Germany was deliberately excluded from the League of Nations, despite having to accept its covenant as part of the Versailles Treaty; this simply hardened the views of those Germans who saw the League as a tool of the Allies rather than as a genuine international organisation. Likewise, the imposition of the disarmament clauses on Germany, which prohibited any kind of air force, reduced the navy to virtual

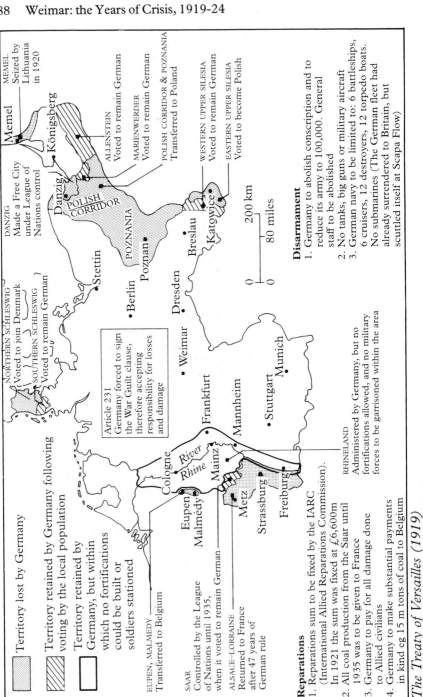

Disarmament

1. Germany to abolish conscription and to reduce its army to 100,000. General staff to be abolished
2. No tanks, big guns or military aircraft
3. German navy to be limited to: 6 battleships, 6 cruisers, 12 destroyers, 12 torpedo boats. No submarines (The German fleet had already surrendered to Britain, but scuttled itself at Scapa Flow)

MEMEL
Seized by Lithuania in 1920

ALLENSTEIN
Voted to remain German

MARIENWERDER
Voted to remain German

POLISH CORRIDOR & POZNANIA
Transferred to Poland

WESTERN UPPER SILESIA
Voted to remain German

EASTERN UPPER SILESIA
Voted to become Polish

DANZIG
Made a Free City under League of Nations control

NORTHERN SCHLESWIG
Voted to join Denmark

SOUTHERN SCHLESWIG
Voted to remain German

Article 231
Germany forced to sign the War Guilt clause, therefore accepting responsibility for losses and damage

RHINELAND
Administered by Germany, but no fortifications allowed, and no military forces to be garrisoned within the area

200 km

80 miles

Memel
Königsberg
Danzig
POLISH CORRIDOR
Stettin
POZNANIA
Poznan
Breslau
Katowice
Berlin
Dresden
Weimar
Frankfurt
Mannheim
Stuttgart
Munich
River Rhine
Cologne
Mainz
Metz
Strassburg
Freiburg
Eupen
Malmédy

Territory lost by Germany

Territory retained by Germany following voting by the local population

Territory retained by Germany, but within which no fortifications could be built or soldiers stationed

EUPEN, MALMEDY
Transferred to Belgium

SAAR
Controlled by the League of Nations until 1935, when it voted to remain German

ALSACE-LORRAINE
Returned to France after 47 years of German rule

Reparations

1. Reparations sum to be fixed by the IARC (International Allied Reparations Commission). In 1921 the sum was fixed at £6,600m
2. All coal production from the Saar until 1935 was to be given to France
3. Germany to pay for all damage done to Allied civilians
4. Germany to make substantial payments in kind eg 15 m tons of coal to Belgium

The Treaty of Versailles (1919)

insignificance and limited the army to a defensive capacity, were seen as grossly unfair when the Allies had in the end made no legally binding commitments to disarm. In the years 1919-45 such views were almost universally held to be true in Germany. In Britain (though not in France where the treaty was generally condemned for being too lenient) a growing sympathy for the German position evolved which laid the basis for the appeasement policy of the 1930s. It was only after the Second World War that the Treaty of Versailles came to be viewed in less polemical terms and a more historical perspective emerged. As a result, historians now tend to portray the peacemakers of 1919 in a more sympathetic light and earlier German criticisms are not so readily accepted.

Of course, Allied statesmen were motivated by their desire to advance their own national interests, and those from France, Belgium and Britain were particularly keen to achieve this at the expense of Germany. However, it is now recognised that it was above all the 'irreparable circumstances' (Schulz) created by the war which framed the peace, rather than naked anti-Germanism. Allied aims and objectives differed in emphasis quite markedly and the difficulty in achieving consensus was compounded by the extraordinarily difficult and complex circumstances of the time. It should be remembered that the Paris peace settlement was not solely concerned with Germany and that numerous other problems had to be dealt with. For example, Britain had vital national interests to uphold in the Middle East arising from the collapse of the Turkish Empire, whilst all the Allies were profoundly concerned by the perceived threat of Soviet Russia and were therefore to varying degrees motivated by desires to contain the Bolshevik menace.

The Treaty of Versailles was in the end a compromise. It was not the Wilsonian peace envisaged by many Germans, but equally it was not nearly so severe as certain sections of Allied opinion had demanded. France had been forced to give way over most of its more extreme demands, such as the creation of an independent Rhineland and the annexation of the Saar. Thus, much of the contemporary German criticism was emotional rhetoric inflamed by years of nationalist propaganda and the shock of defeat. The application of self-determination was not nearly so unfair as many Germans believed. Alsace-Lorraine would have voted for France anyway; plebiscites were held in Schleswig, Silesia and parts of Prussia and as a result frontiers amended; Danzig's status under the League grew logically out of Wilson's promise to provide Poland with access to the sea; whilst the eastern provinces of Posen and West Prussia were rather more mixed in their ethnic make-up than many Germans were prepared to accept. And finally, in comparison to the territorial terms of the Treaty of Brest-Litovsk imposed by Germany on eastern Europe, the Treaty of Versailles appears relatively moderate.

However, the historical significance of the Treaty of Versailles goes well beyond the debate over its 'fairness'. Even more crucial is the issue of its impact upon the young republic. Was Versailles a serious handicap to the establishment of long-term stability in Weimar Germany and if so, how significant was it in its eventual demise?

In terms of the actual political and economic constraints imposed by Versailles, it is no longer tenable to maintain that the treaty was excessively burdensome. As will be seen in the course of the next two chapters, Weimar's economic problems certainly cannot be blamed on the imposition of reparations alone, whilst Germany's perceived loss of status in 1919 was illusory, for in some respects it was in a relatively stronger position than in 1914. The great empires of Russia, Austria-Hungary and Turkey had gone, creating a power vacuum in central and eastern Europe which could not be filled by a weak and isolated USSR or by the generally unstable successor states. In such a situation, a cautious long-term diplomatic policy would probably have led to the establishment of German power and influence at the heart of Europe. Objectively speaking then, Versailles should not be interpreted as a significant constraint on Weimar's successful development. However, on another level Versailles was rather more instrumental, for in the minds of many Germans it was genuinely perceived as the real cause of the country's problems. As a result the Treaty of Versailles developed into a vital propaganda theme with which the anti-republican movement was able to attack the Weimar system. And even for sympathetic democrats, like Hugo Preuss, Versailles only served to disillusion many into thinking that the gains of the revolution were being undone. He wrote in 1923:

1 ... one must first weigh the tremendous obstacles which are being
  put in the path of the new constitution from abroad. The
  suspicious foreign countries have the least right of all to level such
  criticism at our internal development; for the most important
5 cause of all those obstacles is the illegal maltreatment of the
  national democracy by the victors over the Prussian Kaiserdom. If
  the latter was born out of the brilliance of victory, the German
  Republic was born out of its terrible defeat. This difference in
  origin cast from the first a dark shadow on the new political order,
10 as far as national sentiment was concerned; but initially the belief
  still predominated that the new order was necessary for the rebirth
  of Germany. That is why the democratic clauses of the Weimar
  constitution met with relatively little resistance, despite the
  unrivalled severity of the armistice terms. For everyone still
15 expected a peace settlement in accordance with Wilson's 14
  Points, which all the belligerent countries had bindingly accepted
  as the basis for the peace. This would have left the new Germany
  with the political and economic chance to survive and gradually
  pull itself up again, instead of turning it into the pariah among

20 European nations by malevolently draining its national life-blood. The criminal madness of the Versailles *Diktat* was a shameless blow in the face to such hopes based on international law and political common sense. The Reich constitution was born with this
25 curse upon it. That it did not collapse immediately under the strain is striking proof of the intrinsic vitality of its basic principles; but its implementation and evolution were inevitably fatefully restricted and lamed thereby ...

The victorious powers, and France especially, justify their policy
30 of endlessly beating down Germany with the argument that the weakness of the Republic and the strength of its reactionary and nihilistic enemies do not permit confidence to arise in the durability of the new order; and yet it is precisely this policy which has done everything and left nothing undone to weaken the
35 German Republic and strengthen its enemies by destroying the belief that Germany could resurrect itself on the basis of the new constitution.

In this way the Treaty of Versailles became an integral part of the internal political and economic conflict which evolved in Germany after 1919.

2 The Economic and Social Crisis, 1919-23

Not only was the young republic confronted in its early months by the problems of Versailles and the creation of a new constitution, but from the very start it was also saddled with the economic legacy bequeathed by the *Kaiserreich* and the war. A lack of capital for investment, a large trade deficit and the difficulties of readjusting a war economy to the requirements of peace were certainly not helped by demands for reparations from the Allies and the loss of important industrial regions by the Treaty of Versailles. However, the crux of Germany's economic predicament was the massive government deficit and the resulting declining value of the mark which was reflected in the increasing problem of domestic inflation. Between 1913 and 1919 the national debt had risen from 5,000 million marks to 144,000 million marks. Over the same period the value of the mark against the dollar had fallen from 4.20 marks to 14.00 marks and the prices of basic goods had increased three to four fold.

By 1923 Germany's economy was caught in a spiral of hyper-inflation in which figures and values became totally meaningless. It is one of those historical episodes where anecdotal evidence has come to dominate our perceptions:

Wholesale Prices Index, 1913-23 (1913 = 1)

1913	1.00
1918	2.17
1919	4.15
1920	14.86
1921	19.11
1922	341.82
1923 (Jan)	2783.00
1923 (Dec)	1261,000,000,000.00

1 You went into a cafe and ordered a cup of coffee at the prices shown on the blackboard over the service hatch: an hour later, when you asked for the bill, it had gone up by a half or even doubled ... Bartering became more and more widespread.
5   Professional people including lawyers accepted food in preference to cash fees. A haircut cost a couple of eggs, and craftsmen such as watchmakers displayed in their shop windows: 'Repairs carried out in exchange for food'. Once I was asked at the box-office of our local fleapit cinema if I could bring some coal as
10 the price of two seats ... A student I knew had sold his gallery ticket at the State Opera for one dollar to an American; he could live on that money for a whole week. The most dramatic changes in Berlin's outward appearance were the masses of beggars in the streets ... The hardcore of the street markets were the petty black
15 marketeers ... In the summer of that inflation year my grandmother found herself unable to cope. So she asked one of her sons to sell her house. He did so for I don't know how many millions of marks. The old woman decided to keep the money under her mattress and buy food with it as the need arose - with the result that nothing was
20 left except a pile of worthless paper when she died a few months later.

The purpose of the sections is to explain the real causes of Germany's inflation and to assess its social and economic consequences with particular reference to the question of who gained and who lost from the episode.

a) The Causes

For many contemporaries in Weimar Germany the 1923 inflation was beyond rational comprehension. Life became so desperate and so chaotic that simplistic explanations focusing on the financial greed and corruption of the Jews or the detrimental consequences of the Versailles Treaty abounded. Moreover, the incredible experiences of 1923 itself blinded many to the fact that prices had started to rise as far back as 1914. For it is now clear that any explanation of the hyper-inflation cannot be limited to an analysis of 1923 alone but must be rooted in the inflationary spiral initiated by the onset of war in 1914. Germany had made no financial provision for a long drawn out conflict (see page 62) and because of political difficulties the imperial government had refrained from increasing taxation. Instead, it had borrowed massive sums through war bonds and when from 1916 this proved insufficient it had simply continued to allow the national debt to grow. As a result, at a time of almost full employment and high demand, the economy had essentially remained committed to the supply of unproductive weapons of war rather than satisfying the requirements of consumers.

Victory, of course, would have allowed the *Kaiserreich* to recoup its debts by claiming reparations from the Allies, but defeat bequeathed the massive mortgage of the First World War to the Weimar Republic to deal with. By 1919 Germany's finances were in 'an unholy mess' (Berghahn) and the republican government was in an unenviable quandary. Narrowing the massive gap between government income and expenditure and thereby bringing about the control of inflation and the stabilisation of the currency could only be achieved by increasing taxation and/or cutting expenditure. In the light of Germany's internal situation neither of these options was particularly attractive, since both would alienate support for the young republic, depress the economy and increase unemployment. Consequently, from 1919 the new republic continued to pursue a policy of deficit financing, believing that it would enable Germany to overcome the problems of demobilisation whilst also reducing the real value of its internal debt. In this way the inflationary trend was perpetuated.

Therefore, the reparations issue should be seen as a contributory factor to the inflation and not as a primary cause. When the reparations sum was finally fixed by the Reparations Commission at £6,600 million (132 billion *gold* marks), it simply added to the economic burden facing the Weimar government which, rather than tackling the fundamental economic problem of currency instability, proceeded to print money and then sell it on the foreign exchanges in order to raise the required hard currency. This was not a solution, but merely a temporary expedient with disastrous results, for the mark went into sharp decline and inflation climbed even higher.

Germany had already been permitted the postponement of several reparations instalments at the beginning of 1922 when there was a brief attempt to resolve the crisis on an international level by the calling of the ill-fated Genoa Economic Conference. However, the request for another moratorium in July 1922 marked the onset of the final stage of Germany's inflationary crisis. The French government was by this time in the hands of the nationalist Poincaré, who was determined to secure what he saw as France's rightful claims. Therefore, when the Reparations Commission declared Germany to be in default, French and Belgian troops occupied the Ruhr valley, the industrial heart of Germany, in early 1923. It seems that the invasion did help to unite the nation to some extent in common cause against the Allies, but economically the result was to exacerbate massively the inflationary spiral.

The government embarked on a policy of 'passive resistance'. It urged workers to go on strike and to refuse to co-operate with the French, in return for the continued payment of their wages. At the same time the government was unable to collect taxes from the Ruhr and the French prevented the delivery of coal to the rest of Germany, thus forcing its import. In this situation the government's finances fell into total disarray and the mark collapsed to meaningless levels. By autumn 1923 it cost more to print a note than the note was worth and the *Reichsbank* was forced to use newspaper presses to maintain capacity. The German currency ceased to have any value and Germany reverted in effect to a barter society.

The fundamental cause of the German inflation is to be found in the mismanagement of Germany's internal finances from 1914. So, although the inflationary spiral did not develop at a uniform rate - there were short periods when it did decelerate, for example, in spring 1920 and winter 1920-1 - the process was undoubtedly cumulative. At no time was there a willingness by any of the various German governments to bring spending and borrowing back within reasonable limits. Until the end of 1918 the pressure of military necessity was the justification. In the immediate post-war period high levels of government indebtedness continued to be tolerated because of the social and political difficulties facing the new republic. The imposition of reparations simply exacerbated an already parlous situation, in which the government found it more convenient to print money than to tackle the fundamental problem. By the end of 1922 (i.e. before the French occupation of the Ruhr) hyper-inflation had set in. Thereafter, the government exerted no control on its financial policy, preferring instead to bask in the political glory arising from its policy of 'passive resistance'. It was only when the Reich teetered on the verge of complete collapse in September 1923 that a new coalition government under Stresemann regained the political will to implement an economic policy to control effectively the money supply.

b) Winners and Losers

It has often been claimed that the worst consequence of the inflation was the destruction of the German middle class. Stresemann himself said as much in 1927 and later on it was generally assumed that the reason a large proportion of the middle class voted for the Nazis could be put down to their impoverishment in 1923. In the light of recent historical research such assumptions have come to be questioned and a much more differentiated view has begun to emerge about the impact of the inflation on the middle class as well as the rest of society. Even so, it is important to remember that the following general analysis of the social classes cannot possibly do justice to the range of factors, such as region, age and personal circumstances which could affect an individual.

The key to understanding who gained and who lost from the inflation lies in the nature of an individual's income and degree of indebtedness. Clearly, this could have correlated to certain class characteristics, but it was not necessarily so. So what did this mean in practice? It meant that the real winners were those sections of the community who were able to pay off their debts, mortgages and loans with inflated and worthless money. This obviously worked to the advantage of such groups as businessmen, landowners and homeowners (amongst whom obviously were some members of the middle class). Indeed, those who recognised the situation for what it was, made massive gains by buying more real estate from the naive and desperate. This was particularly true of big business which exploited the cheap credit and inflated profits to create large industrial conglomerations. In this category the most notorious example was Hugo Stinnes who by the end of 1923 controlled twenty per cent of German industry. At the other extreme were the savers and mortgagees (including those millions of purchasers of war bonds) who found that good money had simply been invested or loaned for nothing. Some idea of the impact of the inflation can be gleaned from Remarque's novel *Der Schwarze Obelisk* in which a widow explains the suicide of her husband.

1 It was because of the money. It was in a guaranteed five-year deposit in the bank, and he couldn't touch it. It was the dowry for my daughter from my first marriage. He was the trustee. When he was allowed to withdraw it two weeks ago, it wasn't worth anything
5 any more, and the bridegroom broke off the engagement ... My daughter just cried. He couldn't stand that. He thought it was his fault.

In a similar situation were those living on fixed incomes or welfare support, for example students, the retired and the sick. Most grants and pensions progressively lost value in real terms since the increases generally did not keep up with the pace of inflation.

Between the extremes of profit and loss were to be found the mass of the population. In the countryside farmers coped reasonably well, since food remained in demand and they were less dependent on the money economy for the provision of the necessities of life. Shopkeepers and craftsmen also seem to have done good business, especially if they were prepared to exploit the black market. The wages and salaries of employees are, as usual, the most difficult to interpret. The belief that workers' standard of living continued to decline after 1918 is now generally questioned and it seems that until 1922 the level of real wages continued to increase (though not surpassing pre-war levels). It was only in the chaos of 1923, when the trade unions were unable to negotiate wage settlements which could keep pace with the rate of inflation, that a decline took place. Moreover, for the workers there was the added security provided by the relatively low levels of unemployment. As for salaried officials, white collar workers and public employees, here too, the traditional picture of continuous erosion of income has been shown to be inaccurate. According to Holtfrerich the low-point in real terms was actually in early 1920 and in 1921-2 real gains were made, which were only partially lost in the events of 1923.

The material impact of the Weimar inflation is now the subject of very considerable historical research in Germany and generalised contemporary opinions have begun to be revised, even if at times the debate can appear rather pedantic as economic historians descend into the labyrinth of statistics. As a result our historical understanding has been deepened and broadened and there is now a greater appreciation that historical accuracy is best served by drawing more cautious conclusions. There is little to be gained from a ready made 'tick-list' of winners and losers amongst the social groups, for the historical reality was far more differentiated than previously assumed. Two people from the same social class could be affected in very different ways depending on a host of variables. In particular levels of indebtedness and savings were absolutely crucial to one's material fortune or misfortune. In this instance, therefore, any generalised social analysis (such as the one above) must be carefully qualified by an awareness that the nature and extent of the evidence does not facilitate the drawing-up of clear-cut conclusions.

c) An Unmitigated Disaster?

Traditionally, the German inflation has been portrayed as an economic catastrophe with damaging social consequences which paved the way later on for the collapse of the Weimar Republic and the rise of National Socialism. However, in the 1980s a number of economic historians led by Holtfrerich began to interpret the event more positively. Holtfrerich maintains that in the years up to the end of 1922 Weimar's economic policy amounted to a 'rational strategy ... in the national interest'. His thesis is that by continuing the policy of deficit financing the Weimar Republic was able to maintain economic growth and increase production. Assessed against these criteria the German economy compared very favourably with other European economies which went into post-war recession in 1920-1. So, for example, whereas Britain had an unemployment rate of nearly 17 per cent in 1921, Germany had nearly full employment with only 1.8 per cent unemployed and rising wage levels. Such an unusually high level of economic activity at this time also acted as a major stimulus for investment and large sums, especially from the USA, poured into Germany. Finally, Holtfrerich claims that the policy was not only economically beneficial, but politically unavoidable for the survival and very existence of the Weimar Republic, since any kind of retrenchment policy in the early years would have had the most dire economic and social consequences which would have decisively destabilised the infant democracy.

However, it is difficult to accept Holtfrerich's revisionism except in the narrowest sense. He has been criticised for drawing a line between the period up to 1922 of what might be termed 'good inflation' and the subsequent hyper-inflation of 1923 with all its accompanying problems. This seems a rather artificial and dubious distinction bearing in mind the long-term build up to the great inflation and the cumulative nature of its causes. It also tends to separate the inflation from the drastic measures which were eventually required to solve it. His argument is very much that of an economic historian and is based largely on a study of economic and financial data. Consequently, his interpretation tends to marginalise other important criteria in historical analysis, such as the social and psychological dimensions. Above all it has tended to understate the very real human trauma of the inflation for certain elements of German society. In February 1923 the health minister delivered a speech to the *Reichstag*:

1 Unfortunately, this picture of accelerating and shocking decline in health conditions applies to the whole Reich. In the rural areas where many self-sufficient farmers are able to feed themselves and the difficulties resulting from a great density of population do not
5 exist, conditions seem to be better. But in the towns and in the districts with an industrial mass population, there has been a decided deterioration. Especially hard-hit are the middle-class, those living on small annuities, the widows and the pensioners, who with their modest incomes can no longer afford the most basic
10 necessities at present day prices ...
 It is understandable that under such unhygienic circumstances, health levels are deteriorating ever more seriously. While the figures for the Reich as a whole are not yet available, we do have a preliminary mortality rate for towns with 100,000 or more
15 inhabitants. After having fallen in 1920-1, it has climbed again for the year 1921-2, rising from 12.6 to 13.4 per thousand inhabitants ... edema is reappearing, the so-called war dropsy, which is a consequence of a bad and overly watery diet. There are increases in stomach disorders and food poisoning, which are the result of
20 eating spoiled foods. There are complaints of the appearance of

scurvy, which is a consequence of an unbalanced and improper diet. From various parts of the Reich, reports are coming in about an increase in suicides ... More and more often one finds 'old age' and 'weakness' listed in the official records on the cause of death; 25 these are equivalent to death through hunger.

Even more insidious were the effects on behaviour. Profiteering, crime and prostitution all increased markedly at this time. It has often been suggested that such behavioural trends contributed significantly to the lack of faith in the republican system. Such a connection is of course difficult to prove - it is notoriously difficult for historians to assess the importance of morality and beliefs for the effective functioning of past societies. However, it would be naive to dismiss out of hand the possible effects upon German society of the decline in its traditional and very respectable set of values. At the very least, the loss of some old 'certainties' when the democratic framework was still in its infancy must have exacerbated tensions. Perhaps, even more significantly, when yet another crisis developed at the end of the decade, popular confidence in the ability of Weimar to maintain social stability was eventually lost. In that sense the inflation of 1923 was not the occasion of Weimar's demise, but it left a deep and lasting psychological scar from which Weimar could not disassociate itself.

3 The Political Crisis

However much emphasis one wishes to place on the economic crisis facing Weimar Germany, it still remains true that from the start there were underlying structural problems in the political system which went a lot deeper than the criticisms of the constitutional framework. Despite the relative success of the *Reichstag* elections in January 1919 for the forces sympathetic to the republic, such problems were rooted in the very nature of the Weimar political establishment. The republic was confronted by political opposition from the extreme left and right, whilst its democratic supporters were faced with the ongoing problem of creating and maintaining government coalitions. In the years 1919-24 the cumulative effect of these political problems, exacerbated by the economic context and a nationalistic, predatory France, created an atmosphere of ongoing political crisis which reached its height in the year 1923. Indeed, Kolb goes as far as to claim that Weimar's very survival at this time should be viewed as 'almost a miracle'.

a) Left-wing Opposition

After the revolution of 1918-19 socialist politics remained in a state of confusion (see the table on pages 83-4). The SPD was indisputably committed to parliamentary democracy; the KPD took its lead from

Bolshevik Russia and pressed for proletarian revolution; and the USPD was caught in the middle, pressing for the creation of a socialist society, but within a democratic framework. However, this situation was clarified by the demise in the USPD in 1920 which resulted in its members joining either the KPD (the extreme revolutionary left) or the SPD (the moderate parliamentary left) - and between these two forces the divide was both deep and wide. Why did the extreme left so vehemently oppose the republic and how serious a threat was it to the republic's stability?

The extreme left viewed the establishment of parliamentary democracy as no more than a 'bourgeois compromise'. It wanted the revolution to proceed on Marxist-Leninist lines with the creation of a one-party socialist state and the major restructuring of Germany's social and economic fabric. Its opposition to the republic therefore amounted to a wholesale rejection of the system - it was not prepared to be a 'loyal opposition' and work within the parliamentary system to bring about its desired changes. In this sense the ideological outlook between the moderate and extreme left was so fundamental that there was no chance of political co-operation between them, let alone a *rapprochement* of the socialist movement. The extreme left was wholeheartedly committed to a very different vision of German politics and society whereas the moderate left was one of the key-stones of Weimar democracy.

With hindsight it is clear that the extreme left posed much less of a threat to Weimar than was believed at the time. Its electoral support at 10-15 per cent and more particularly its revolutionary actions, like, for example, the creation of a short-lived soviet republic in Bavaria (April 1919) and the attempted armed uprising in Saxony (March 1921), gave the impression of a 'Red Threat'. It frightened many - prompted also by the propaganda of the extreme right - into exaggerated fears. In particular, it drove the parliamentary left and other democrats into increasing reliance on the forces of reaction. However, the reality was not nearly so threatening. Even during the chaos and uncertainty of 1923 the opposition of the extreme left was limited to several isolated incidents and it proved incapable of mounting a unified attack on Weimar democracy. It had been weakened by its ideological divisions and further uncertainty was created over the tactics it should employ. The repression it endured at the hands of the *Freikorps* (see page 101) also removed some of its ablest and most spirited leaders. The result was that it was never able to gain more than about one-third of the support from the working class. In the end the extreme left was just not powerful enough to lead a revolution against Weimar, although its opposition, together with that of its political antithesis, the extreme right, severely limited Weimar's base of support from the start.

b) Right-wing Opposition

Opposition from the extreme right was very different both in its form and in its extent to that of the extreme left. On the right wing of the political spectrum there was to be found a diverse collection of opponents to the republic and their resistance found expression in very different ways. The threat from the extreme right must therefore be analysed on several levels. What did it stand for? Who or what was the extreme right? And did it pose a more serious threat to the viability of Weimar democracy than the extreme left?

The extreme right was united by its total rejection of the Weimar system and its principles. It sought to destroy the democratic constitution and to establish some kind of authoritarian nationalist regime. Central to this conservative-nationalist opposition was the cultivated belief in the 'Stab-in-the-Back' myth. The war, it was argued, had been lost not because of any military defeat suffered by the army, but as a result of the betrayal of unpatriotic forces within Germany. These were the pacifists, the socialists, the democrats, the Jews - a whole range of scapegoats were used by right-wing politicians to take the blame for accepting the armistice. Worse still these 'November Criminals' had been prepared to overthrow the monarchy and establish a republic, which had added insult to injury by accepting the 'shameful peace' of Versailles. Such distorted interpretations of the events of 1918-19 were universally accepted by the extreme right. They not only served to alleviate the *Kaiserreich* of responsibility, but they also acted as a powerful stick with which to beat the new leaders of Germany.

Manifestations of the extreme right appeared in various guises. It assumed its most overt political form in a number of political parties. It was also the driving-force behind the activities of various para-military terrorist organisations, and it also exerted a pervasive influence in a number of key institutions of the German state.

The DNVP was a coalition of nationalist forces centred around the old imperial conservative parties, but also embracing such groups as the Fatherland Party and the Pan-German League. It therefore contained significant radical and racist elements from the very start, and, although it was still the party of landowners and parts of heavy industry, it had a sufficiently broad social appeal amongst elements of the middle classes to poll 15.1 per cent in the 1920 election. Although the DNVP remained the dominant force on the extreme right until the depression set in at the end of the decade, there were numerous other fringe parties. The emergence of radical *völkisch* nationalism, as has been shown, was clearly apparent before 1914, but the effects of the war and its aftermath acted as a powerful catalyst. Bavaria, in particular, became a haven for such groups, since the state government was sufficiently reactionary to tolerate many of them. One such group was the German Workers' Party which Hitler joined in 1919. However, in the years 1919-24 regional and policy differences divided such groups and attempts to unify the radical nationalist right ended in failure. It was not until the mid-1920s, when Hitler began to absorb the welter of different groups under his leadership of the NSDAP, that a potent electoral force was created

In the early years of the Weimar Republic radical nationalism was more active with the bullet than with the ballot-box. The *Freikorps* units which flourished in the post-war environment were a haven for the more brutal and ugly elements of German militarism. Although they were employed on occasions by the government to suppress the perceived threat from the extreme left, the *Freikorps* were anti-republican and committed to the restoration of authoritarian rule. They exhibited many of the worst features and blind prejudices of the radical right, which they expressed in an arbitrarily violent fashion.

The *Freikorps* were almost certainly behind the gang called 'Organisation Consul' which assassinated the two key republican politicians, Erzberger and Rathenau, and they also played a central role in the first attempt by the right wing to seize power from the constitutional government in the Kapp-Lüttwitz Putsch of 1920. Wolfgang Kapp was a former Prussian civil servant and a founder member of the Fatherland Party, and General Lüttwitz was considered to be 'the father of the *Freikorps*'. In early 1920 the need to reduce the

The White General *by G. Grosz*

size of the German army according to the terms of the Versailles Treaty created considerable unease within the ranks of the *Freikorps*. When it was proposed to dissolve the Ehrhardt Brigade near Berlin, Kapp and Lüttwitz decided to exploit the situation and to march on the capital. Unopposed they entered Berlin and installed a new government which issued the following proclamation:

1 The Reich and the nation are in grave danger. With terrible speed we are approaching the complete collapse of the State and of law and order. The people are only dimly aware of the approaching disaster. Prices are rising unchecked. Hardship is growing.
5 Starvation threatens. Corruption, usury, nepotism and crime are cheekily raising their heads. The government, lacking in authority, impotent and in league with corruption is incapable of overcoming the danger. Away with a government in which Erzberger is the leading light! ...
10 What principles should be our guide? Not reaction, but a free development of the German State, restoration of order and the sanctity of the law. Duty and conscience must reign again in the German land. German honour and honesty must be restored ... The hour of the salvation of Germany is at hand and must be used;
15 therefore there is no other way but a government of action. What are the tasks facing the new government? ...
The government will ruthlessly suppress strikes and sabotage. Everyone should go peacefully about his work. Everyone willing to work is assured of our firm protection: striking is treason to the
20 nation, the Fatherland and the future. The government will ... not be a one-sided capitalist one. It will rather save German workers from the hard fate of slavery to international big business and hopes by such measures to put an end to the hostility of the working classes to the State ... We shall govern not according to
25 theories but according to the practical needs of the State and the nation as a whole. In the best German tradition the State must stand above the conflict of classes and parties. It is the objective arbiter in the present conflict between capital and labour. We reject the granting of class-advantage to the Right or the Left. We
30 recognise only German citizens. Everyone must do his duty! The first duty of every man is to work. Germany must be a moral working community!

Significantly, the army did not provide any resistance to this putsch. Despite requests from Ebert and the chancellor to put down the rebellious forces, the army's attitude was ambivalent. Admittedly it did not throw in its lot with the putschists, but neither did it feel bound to support the country's legitimate government. General von Seeckt, the senior officer in the Defence Ministry, spoke for many colleagues when he declared:

1 Troops do not fire on troops. So, you perhaps intend, Herr
   Minister, that a battle be fought before the Brandenburger Tor
   between troops that have fought side by side against a common
   enemy? When *Reichswehr* fires on *Reichswehr* then all comradeship
5 within the officers corps will have vanished.

The army's decision to put its own institutional interests before its
obligation to defend the government forced the latter to flee the capital
and to withdraw to Stuttgart. However, despite such ignominy, the
putsch rapidly collapsed. Before leaving Berlin, the SPD members of the
government had called for a general strike, which soon paralysed the
capital and quickly spread to the rest of the country. After four days it
was clear that Kapp and his government exerted no real authority and
they fled the city. At first sight the collapse of the Kapp Putsch could be
viewed as a major success for the republic - it had retained the backing of
popular opinion and thereby it had effectively withstood a major threat
from the extreme right. However, it is also surely significant that the
Kapp Putsch had taken place at all! In this sense the Kapp Putsch
highlights all too clearly the weakness of the Weimar Republic in the face
of the nation's institutions. Their behaviour in the putsch was
symptomatic of their right-wing attitudes and their lack of sympathy for
the republic and its principles. In the months after the coup the
government failed to confront this problem.

The army leadership, for example, had clearly revealed its dubious
reliability. Yet, amazingly, Seeckt himself was appointed Chief of the
Army Command at the end of that very month - an appointment made
on the dubious logic that he enjoyed the confidence of his fellow officers
and ignoring the fact that his attitude to the republic was at best
luke-warm. Under Seeckt's influence (1920-6) the army was turned into
a 'state within a state' (Scheidemann) with a privileged position which
placed it in effect beyond direct democratic accountability. Many within
its ranks believed that the army served some higher purpose to the
nation as a whole and therefore it had the right to intervene as it saw fit
without regard to its obligations to the republic.

The judiciary likewise perpetuated anachronistic political values
which reflected the conservative authoritarianism of imperial times. It
doubted the legitimacy and principles of the new republic and this made
for an irregular and dubious application of justice. The putschists of
1920 never felt the full rigour of the law: Kapp died in prison awaiting
trial; Lüttwitz was granted early retirement; and even those who were
brought to trial were sentenced to only five years imprisonment. Such
treatment was not untypical. After the Munich Beer Hall Putsch of
1923, Hitler was sentenced to a mere five years, but was released after
less than 12 months, and Ludendorff was acquitted altogether. In

contrast, leaders of left-wing uprisings faced lengthy prison sentences or even the death penalty. There is no doubt that the judiciary was politically biased in favour of the extreme right and, strengthened by its right of professional security its judgements served to weaken the republic and embolden the right-wing opposition. Much the same could also be said for other key institutions such as the civil service and the educational establishment.

The depth and extent of the opposition from the extreme right to Weimar was not always fully appreciated. It ranged from indifference to brutal violence, but ironically because of the perceived threat from the extreme left, the republican regime came to rely on the forces of reaction, particularly in the spheres of justice and law and order. In many respects it was this persistence of the old attitudes and the lack of real support for democracy in the institutions which represented the greatest long-term threat to Weimar. The more violent forces of counter-revolution, as shown by the putsches of Kapp and Hitler, were at this time actually too weak and disorganised to seize power. It was a lesson Hitler himself came to appreciate as he languished in gaol during 1924.

4 How and Why did Weimar Survive the Years of Crisis?

In 1923 Weimar's political and economic crisis came to a head. French and Belgian troops occupied the Ruhr and with no effective means to oppose them the German government resorted to the policy of 'passive resistance'. Meanwhile, the German currency collapsed and hyper-inflation set in. As a result, various political disturbances took place across the country culminating in an attempted Communist uprising in Saxony and the failed Hitler putsch in Bavaria. The republic was very close to dissolution. Yet, only a few months later a semblance of calm and normality had returned. Peukert's telling comment that 1923 shows 'there are no entirely hopeless situations in history' is not only indicative of Weimar's remarkable survival but also the difficulty for historians in explaining it.

It is certainly important to recognise that decisive political action was taken in the second half of 1923 to confront the crisis and that the results were undoubtedly beneficial. From the end of 1922 things had just been allowed to slide, but the appointment of Gustav Stresemann as chancellor in August 1923 (see page 122) witnessed the emergence of a politician who was actually prepared to take difficult decisions in an attempt to resolve Germany's economic plight and international impotence. Stresemann called off 'passive resistance' and promised to resume the payment of reparations. He also sharply reduced government expenditure so as to cut the deficit, whilst creating a new currency, the *Rentenmark*. The result was an almost miraculous halt to the inflationary cycle, the establishment of a stable currency, and the political basis for international negotiations on Germany's economic plight. The 'miracle of the *Rentenmark*' and Stresemann's conciliatory policy gained Germany some sympathy from the Allies, and the Dawes Committee was established to examine Germany's financial position. Its report, the Dawes Plan, published in April 1924, did not reduce the overall reparations bill, but for the first five years geared the payments directly to Germany's economic capacity and provided for a large international loan. The acceptance of the Dawes Plan by both Germany and the Allies can be seen to mark the beginning of a new era both in international relations and in Germany's domestic condition.

Although Stresemann's resolute action in tackling the problems might help to explain why the years of crisis came to an end, on its own it does not really help us to understand why Weimar was able to come through the years of crisis. Weimar's survival in 1923 was in marked contrast to its ignominious collapse a decade later. Why was this? Why did Weimar not collapse in the crisis-ridden months before Stresemann's emergence on the political scene? Here the explanatory analysis is not so clear-cut and conclusions must be tempered by a large degree of caution. It is another case of where historians and their students have to admit the limits of historical certainty!

It could be argued, for example, that popular resentment was channelled more towards the French and the Allies than towards Weimar itself. It has also been suggested that, despite the effects of inflation, workers did not suffer to the same extent as they did when there was long-term mass unemployment. Similarly, employers tended to show a less hostile attitude to Weimar in its early years than in its final phase of deflationary economic depression (and, of course, some businessmen did very well out of the inflation). If some or all of these assumptions about popular instincts towards Weimar are valid, then it seems that, although there was distress and disillusionment in 1923, disaffection with Weimar had not yet reached critical proportions (unlike 1932-3). Moreover, in 1923 there was no clear political alternative to Weimar. The extreme left had not really recovered from its divisions and suppression in the years 1918-21 and in its isolated position it did not enjoy enough support to overthrow Weimar. The extreme right too was not yet strong enough - it was divided and with no clear strategy. The failure of the Kapp Putsch served as a clear warning of the dangers of precipitate action - and was probably the main reason why the army did not take the initiative in 1923.

The Weimar Republic therefore survived its post-war years of crisis. It is worth remembering at this stage that other regimes did not fare so well - Italy (a liberal democracy since 1870) and Hungary were already moving towards dictatorship and Poland soon followed. Weimar democracy can hardly then be described as merely 'a fair weather system'. In 1923 it had managed to withstand a major storm. Was this a sign of real political strength and credibility? If so, perhaps it could build on its advantages as it moved into the calmer waters of the mid-1920s?

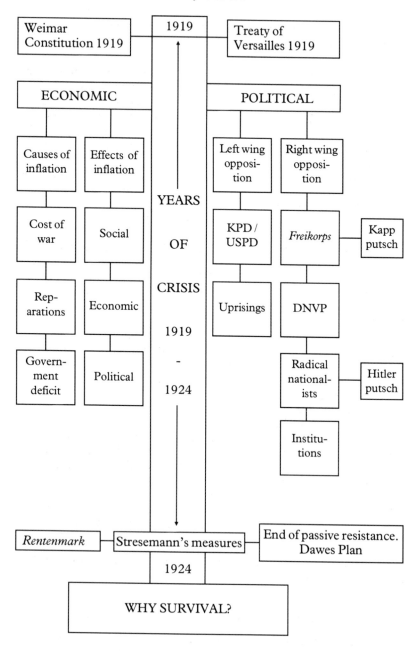

Summary - Weimar: the Years of Crisis, 1919-24

Making notes on 'Weimar: the Years of Crisis'

There is a lot of ground to be covered in this chapter both in terms of content and analysis and a good understanding is essential. Not only could the material form the basis of an essay question in its own right, but it is also vital for a proper appreciation of the later history of Weimar. In addition, it ties in with other topics you will probably study in your outline course - e.g., the peace settlement and the post-war crisis - where comparisons between Germany and Italy are particularly relevant. So, at least you should feel that your note-taking is worthwhile! The following headings should provide a suitable framework for your notes.

1.   The Constitution and Peace Treaty
1.1 The Weimar constitution. List and explain the main issues of controversy in the constitution.
1.2 Versailles Treaty. Draw the map on page 88. Explain which parts of the Versailles Treaty were resented most in Germany. Look back at your notes in the last section. Did the peace treaty or the constitution have the more detrimental effect on Weimar's evolution? Explain your answer.
2.   The Economic Crisis
2.1 Causes. Long-term; medium-term; and short-term.
2.2 Effects. Draw a spider-diagram and include as many effects as possible. Re-order your points under four headings: disastrous; serious; tolerable; beneficial. Was the Great Inflation really an unmitigated disaster?
3.   The Political Crisis
3.1 Left-wing opposition. Why did the extreme left fail to bring about communist revolution in Germany during the years of crisis?
3.2 Right-wing opposition. Identify clearly the breadth of the opposition from the extreme right. Why did the extreme right fail to topple Weimar democracy during the years of crisis?
4.   The Survival of Weimar Democracy
4.1 Stresemann's action. Possible reasons for Weimar's survival. Can you think of any other factors which might explain Weimar's survival at this time?

It will be necessary to return to this chapter and the issues raised by it at the end of Chapter 7.

Answering essay questions on "Weimar: The Years of Crisis'

Sometimes the analytical focus of a question is contained in one key word or phrase. Examine the following questions and decide upon the key word(s) in each case:

1. To what extent was Germany crippled by the Treaty of Versailles?
2. How far would you agree that Weimar's early problems were fundamentally economic?
3. How accurate is it to describe Weimar's survival in 1923 as a miracle?
4. To what extent were Germany's problems in the years of crisis, 1919-23, caused by external forces?
5. Would you agree that the threat to Weimar democracy from the extreme left in the years 1918-23 was only a mirage?

You probably had little trouble identifying the key words - though you might have been lured by the word 'crisis' in question 4 when actually the focus for discussion is whether 'external forces' (as opposed to internal pressures) created the crisis. But clearly it is not enough just to identify the key word/phrase in a question. You must also be able to understand exactly what it means and to appreciate its implications. For example, in question 5 the key word is 'mirage', but are you aware of how it is inviting you to distinguish between the image and the reality of Weimar's situation? If you are writing an essay as part of your course work, then this sort of problem should present no problem because you have the time and the opportunity to think it through. But if you are in the examination room, you would be well-advised to keep clear of any question where the key word/phrase is not clear in your own mind.

Such questions often invite you to gauge the extent of your agreement. Hence, the opening phrases: 'how far'; 'to what extent' etc. If this is the case, then you will need to create an essay structure in two main parts. The first part will examine the points in favour of the proposition and the second part will discuss those against it. Finally, a conclusion should show the reader what you believe the answer to be on balance. Remember that history is more often a subtle shade of grey rather than black or white and your conclusion should try to give an idea of where you stand on the historical spectrum. With these points in mind construct an essay-plan for question 4 and then draft a conclusion.

Source-based questions on 'Weimar: the Years of Crisis'

1 The Constitution

Read the extracts from T. Heuss and H. Preuss on pages 86-7 and 90-1. Answer the following questions.

a) Explain the following references: i) 'Stab-in-the-Back' Myth (1 mark); ii) 'Wilson's 14 Points' (1 mark); and iii) 'the illegal maltreatment of the national democracy by the victors over the Prussian Kaiserdom'. (2 marks)
b) What evidence do the extracts contain to suggest that they were written by democrats? (2 marks)

c) Explain how the historical circumstances in which each extract was written might have affected their objectivity. (4 marks)
d) Was the internal development of the republic most adversely affected by the Weimar Constitution or by the Versailles Treaty? (5 marks)

2 The Great Inflation

Study the table on page 92 and then carefully read the extracts on pages 92, 95 and 97-8. Answer the following questions.
a) Explain the following references: 'black marketeers'; 'annuities'; 'wholesale prices'. (3 marks)
b) With reference to the health report describe and explain the impact of the inflation on the nation's health. (5 marks)
c) What is the value, if any, to a historian of Weimar Germany of a novel and a collection of anecdotal memories? Explain your answer with reference to the extracts from Remarque and Larsen. (4 marks)
d) 'The detrimental effects of the great inflation have been grossly exaggerated.' Do these sources and other evidence known to you support this assertion? (8 marks)

3 The Kapp Putsch

Study the drawing, 'The White General' on page 101 and read carefully the proclamation of the Kapp government and the statement of Seeckt on pages 102-3. Answer the following questions.
a) What image is Grosz trying to project in his drawing of the *Freikorps* officer? (4 marks)
b) Why does Grosz entitle the drawing 'The White General'? What does this imply about Grosz's own political attitudes? (4 marks)
c) How does the proclamation of the Kapp government try to justify the *putsch*? How does Seeckt try to justify the army's inaction? (4 marks)
d) In what ways does the proclamation try to appeal for support from different sections of the population? (3 marks)
e) What are the implications of the new government's declared aim that 'it shall govern not ... class and parties'? (4 marks)
f) How far do these sources explain the reasons for Weimar's weaknesses in its early years? (6 marks)

CHAPTER 6

Weimar: Relative Stability, 1924-9

The years 1924-9 have traditionally been regarded as the high point of the Weimar Republic - a glorious, albeit short-lived, interlude between the early years of crisis and its eventual decline and collapse during the Depression. It has been seen as a time when the cliché of 'the golden twenties' actually seems to have had a ring of truth about it. William Shirer, the American journalist, described his first impressions of Germany at this time:

1 I was stationed in Paris and occasionally in London at that time, and fascinating though those capitals were ... they paled a little when one came to Berlin and Munich. A wonderful ferment was working in Germany. Life seemed more free, more modern, more
5 exciting than in any place I had ever seen. Nowhere else did the arts or the intellectual life seem so lively. In contemporary writing, painting, architecture, in music and drama, there were new currents and fine talents. And everywhere there was an accent on youth ... They were a healthy, carefree, sunworshipping lot, and
10 they were filled with an enormous zest for living life to the full and in complete freedom. The old oppressive Prussian spirit seemed to be dead and buried. Most Germans one met - politicians, writers, editors, artists, professors, students, businessmen, labour leaders - struck you as being democratic, liberal, even pacifist.

The popular rosy image of Weimar in the mid-1920s is not without some substance, since comparatively this middle period achieved a number of notable successes. However, historians have increasingly come to question the real extent of Weimar's health and stability at this time, bearing in mind that it disintegrated so soon after the onset of the world depression.

1 Economic Recovery?

It is often maintained that the stabilisation of the currency and the implementation of the Dawes Plan ushered in five years of economic growth and affluence, which stands out in marked contrast to the inflationary chaos of 1922-3, and which was only brought to an end by the world depression of 1929-33. Certainly, for many contemporaries looking back from the standpoint of the end of the 1920s it seemed as if Germany had made a remarkable recovery. In 1929 the economist W.A. Angell published an influential book entitled *The Recovery of Germany*. Gilbert Parker, the American financier and the Agent for Reparation Payments, had reported to the Reparations Commission in December 1928:

1 German business conditions generally appear to have righted themselves on a relatively high level of activity. A year ago, it will be recalled, German business was in the midst of a process of expansion which threatened to result in over-production in certain 5 of the principal industries ... As the year 1928 comes to a close, it appears that this over-expansion has been checked before it reached dangerous proportions, and that a condition of relative stability has now been attained ... Since 1924, when stabilisation was achieved and the execution of the Experts' Plan began, 10 Germany's reconstruction has at least kept pace with the reconstruction of Europe as a whole, and it has played an essential part in the process of European reconstruction.

Heavy industry, despite its loss of resources arising from Versailles, was able to recover reasonably quickly and by 1928 production levels generally exceeded those of 1913. This was the result of more efficient production techniques, particularly in coal-mining and steel manufacture, and also the large-scale investment of foreign capital into this sector. Foreign investors were attracted to Germany because of its relatively high interest rates. At the same time German industry achieved economies of scale by the growing number of cartels. IG Farben, the chemicals giant, became the largest manufacturing enterprise in Europe and Vereinigte Stahlweeke combined the coal, iron and steel interests of Germany's great industrial magnates so as to control nearly half of all production. Between 1925 and 1929 exports rose by 40 per cent. Such economic progress was reflected in social terms as well. Hourly wages rose in real terms every year from 1924 to 1930 and by as much as five per cent and ten per cent in 1927 and 1928. There were also striking improvements in the provision of social welfare: a generous pensions and sickness benefits scheme was implemented; in 1927 compulsory unemployment insurance covering 17 million workers (the largest of its kind in the world) was introduced; and state subsidies were provided for the construction of local amenities - parks, schools, sports facilities and especially council housing. All these developments alongside the more overt signs of affluence, such as the increasing number of cars and the growth of the cinema, gave support to the view that the Weimar economy was enjoying boom conditions.

In actual fact the rapidity of German recovery was deceptive. There was indeed economic growth, but it was far from even and in 1926 production actually declined. The balance of trade was consistently in the red. Unemployment never fell below 1.3 million in this period and even before the shock-waves of America's financial crisis began to be felt it was averaging 1.9 million during 1929. Meanwhile, in the agricultural sector, grain production was still only three-quarters of its 1913 figure and farmers, already often in debt, faced declining incomes. By the late 1920s per capita income in agriculture was 44 per cent below the national average. What were the reasons for these economic problems and were they so serious as to represent a long-term threat to the health of the German economy?

Firstly, world economic conditions did not favour a country like Germany which had traditionally depended on its export capacity for growth. World trade did not return to pre-war levels and, inhibited further by growing protectionism, German exports as a share of GNP declined (Germany's export capacity was also limited by the loss of valuable territories such as Alsace-Lorraine and Silesia by the Versailles Treaty). German agriculture also found itself in dire straits because of world conditions. The fall in world prices from the mid-1920s was placing a great strain on farmers who actually made up one-third of the population. Subsidies and tariffs could only partially alleviate the problems and anyway they in turn were likely to create additional economic and political burdens. Most significantly, the marked decline in the income of such a sizeable section of the population contributed to a contraction in demand within the economy as a whole. A further circumstantial problem was the changing balance of the population. From the mid-1920s those who were part of the pre-war baby-boom began to come on to the labour market, thus increasing the available work-force from 32.4 million in 1925 to 33.4 million in 1931. Even without recession, it was always likely that there were going to be relatively higher levels of unemployment. Rates of investment and savings were also not encouraging. Savers had lost a great deal of money in the post-war inflation and after 1924 there was little confidence to commit money again. Starved of investment capital the German economy came to rely on investors from abroad, who were attracted by the prospect of higher interest rates on short-term deposit than they could earn from long-term deposit in their own countries. As a result, Germany's economic well-being became even more dependent on and vulnerable to the investment whims of foreign capital. Government finances were likewise a cause for grave concern. Although the government succeeded in balancing the budget in 1924, from 1925 it continually ran deficits whilst at the same time continuing to expand its financial commitments. By 1928 public expenditure had reached 26 per cent of GNP - double the pre-war figure - and the government, unable to offset the deficit by encouraging domestic savings, was increasingly forced to rely on international loans. Such a situation did not provide the basis for sound economic growth as some contemporary observers readily recognised. In its annual report of 1927 the Deutsche Bank said:

There can in fact be no question of any steady development of our economic life as long as the Reparations problem has not been solved definitively and in a manner favourable to us.

In 1928 it referred to,

1 ... the complete inner weakness of our economy. It is so overloaded
with taxes required by the excessively expensive apparatus of the
state, with over-high social payments, and particularly with the
reparations sum now reaching its 'normal' level [as laid down by
5 the Dawes Plan] that any healthy growth is constricted.
Development is only possible to the extent that these restrictive
chains are removed.

All this suggests that the German economy was already in a highly
precarious condition even before the onset of the depression. At the time
the problems were effectively masked by the massive influx of foreign
capital and by the development of an extensive, but costly, social welfare
system. Yet, both these factors were in their own way 'time-bombs'
waiting to go off. What remains less clear-cut is the depth of Weimar's
economic malaise in this middle period, and whether its condition
should be considered as terminal for the viability of democracy.

In the late 1970s the Munich economic historian Borchardt was the
first to argue that during the years 1925-9 Germany was living well
beyond its means and that its economy was chronically sick. Not only
were public finances out of control, but wage levels were rising
excessively without taking sufficient account of actual productivity.
This, he maintained, was the result of government intervention in the
labour market which generally exhibited an overly sympathetic attitude
towards organised labour. For example, the introduction of compulsory
wage arbitration and the higher employer contributions for social
insurance both increased production costs which led to lower
investment and sluggish economic growth. By 1927-8 expectations of
declining profitability had so adversely affected the business climate that
already the 'points were set to depression'. His assessment of the
Weimar economy concluded that it was an 'abnormal, in fact a sick
economy, which could not possibly have gone on in the same way, even
if the world depression had not occurred'.

Borchardt's thesis has proved to be a controversial one. At a time
when the world was again in the midst of economic recession and when a
fierce debate raged between Keynesian and monetarist economists,
Borchardt's interpretation had a particular resonance to it. Not
surprisingly, therefore, his views have not found universal acceptance. A
strong rearguard action has been fought by Holtfrerich who has
maintained that the economy's condition was far from chronic and was
in actual fact only temporarily 'off the rails'. He has thrown doubt on
Borchardt's analysis of statistical evidence and he has particularly
questioned the view that excessive wage pressure was at the heart of
Weimar's economic problems. Labour income should be seen as more
of a symptom of business conditions than a cause, he claims. Instead,
the crux of Weimar's economic malaise was to be found in the high level
of German interest rates which discouraged industrial and agricultural

investment, but still failed to restore the population's faith in savings. Consequently, investment and growth remained at low levels and the creation of new jobs was poor.

It is now generally recognised that by 1929 the Weimar economy was facing serious problems as a result of both external forces and severe internal structural problems. Indeed, it seems safe to draw two key conclusions. Firstly, the German economy's dependence on foreign loans made it dangerously susceptible to the shock-waves from any future dislocation in the world economic system. And secondly, various sectors of the German economy had actually started to go into recession from 1927. Whether this amounts to proof of Borchardt's thesis of a 'sick' economy, however, remains more controversial. Any assessment of how events would have unfolded without the world economic crisis is, of course, speculative. However, on balance the evidence tends to suggest that Weimar's economic condition by 1929 was so parlous that it was already in the throes of economic crisis. In that sense the Weimar economy experienced a 'crisis before the crisis' and America's financial collapse - although of vital importance - actually only exacerbated an already grave situation.

2 Political Recovery?

An analysis of the election results in the middle period of the Weimar Republic suggests grounds for cautious optimism about its long-term survival (see the results for 1924 and 1928 in the table on page 140). The extremist parties of both left and right generally lost ground and altogether polled less than 30 per cent of the votes cast. The DNVP peaked in December 1924 with 103 seats (20.5 per cent) and fell back to 73 (14.2 per cent) in May 1928. The Nazis lost ground in both elections and were reduced to 12 seats (2.6 per cent) by 1928. And the KPD, although recovering slightly by 1928 with 54 seats (10.6 per cent), remained below the performance of May 1924 (and well below the combined performance of the KPD and USPD in June 1920). On the other hand, the parties sympathetic to the republic generally maintained their share of the vote or, as in the case of the SPD, made substantial improvements, gaining 153 seats (29.8 per cent) in 1928. Consequently, in the wake of the 1928 election a 'Grand Coalition' of the SPD, DDP, DVP and Centre was formed. It was led by Hermann Müller of the SPD and it enjoyed the support of over 60 per cent of the *Reichstag*. It seemed as if a democratic consensus was at last beginning to emerge in Weimar politics.

However, not only must the election of 1928 be regarded as atypical of Weimar history, but it should also not be allowed to disguise the continuing fundamental weaknesses of the parliamentary and party system. These were not the system of proportional representation or the concept of coalition government, but rather the ongoing dilemma of creating coalitions from the main parties and then maintaining them when individual party interests remained especially strong. The parties continued to reflect their traditional interest of religious denomination or class and attempts to widen their appeal had made little headway. As a result the differences between the main parties were so fundamental that the possible combinations within a coalition were actually very limited. There was never any possibility of a coalition including both the SPD and the DNVP, and the KPD remained totally isolated, so the only options available were: a right-centre coalition of Centre, DVP and DNVP, which tended to agree on domestic issues, but disagree on foreign affairs; a broad coalition of SPD, DDP DVP and Centre which could agree on foreign policy but had very different domestic agenda; and finally, a minority government of the political centre, including the DDP, DVP and Centre, but seeking support from left or right as required. In effect, it was impossible to create a coalition with a parliamentary majority which could also consistently agree on both domestic and foreign policy. In this situation, there was very little real chance of democratic government being able to establish any long-term political stability. Of the seven governments between 1924 and 1930 only two boasted majorities and the longest survived 21 months. In fact, the only reason governments lasted as long as they did was because of the inability or the unwillingness of the opposition to unite. More often than not it was the ever-changing shifts of power within the parties of government which actually led to collapse.

The attitude of Weimar's political parties towards parliamentary government was really rather naive and irresponsible. This may well have been a legacy from imperial times when their limited constitutional role had allowed them the privilege of advancing narrow sectional interests in the knowledge that the executive was only responsible to the emperor. However, parliamentary democracy necessitated a much more compromising and responsible attitude towards government - and on the whole the evidence from even the most stable phase of Weimar's history suggests that such an attitude had not evolved.

For example, the SPD, the strongest party in the *Reichstag* until 1932, and by reputation the mainstay of republicanism, remained divided between its wish to uphold the interests of the working class and its commitment to democracy. Some, particularly those on the left and those affiliated to the strong trade union influence in the party, feared that accommodation with the bourgeois liberal parties would lead to the dilution of the party's socialist programme. Others, of more moderate views, urged participation in government in order to guarantee it remaining in sympathetic hands. At the same time the old ideological argument between the reformists and the theoretical Marxists (see page 23) continued to dog the party. As a result, the SPD found itself in a 'defensive position' during the middle period of the republic and amazingly it did not even join any of the government coalitions until

1928. And then almost immediately Müller, the SPD chancellor, faced a condemnatory motion from his own party because the coalition had backed the construction of one armoured cruiser!

It therefore fell to the Centre Party to provide the political lead and to some extent it did fulfil that role. The Centre backed all the governments from 1919 to 1932 and it held ministerial posts in most. However, its attempts to bridge the social classes and to extend its appeal beyond its denominational base not only had very limited success but also contributed to internal divisions over social and economic policy. In the early years, such differences had been effectively put to one side under the clear, but leftish, leadership of Erzberger and Wirth. However, during the 1920s the Party moved decisively to the right and the fissures within became increasingly apparent. In 1928 the leadership eventually passed to Kaas and Brüning for whom conservative and authoritarian political partners had rather more appeal than coalition with the forces of liberalism or social democracy - a worrying sign for the future of the Centre and Germany itself.

The position of German liberalism also left a great deal to be desired. Admittedly, the DDP and DVP participated in all the coalition governments of this period and in Stresemann, the leader of the DVP and the republic's one real statesman, liberalism had a continuous source of influence and inspiration. However, none of this could hide some worrying trends. Their share of the vote, though remaining reasonably constant in this middle period, had nearly halved since 1919-20, when it had been between 22 and 23 per cent. The seeds of liberalism's eventual disintegration after 1930 had already clearly been sown. This decline was largely a reflection of the factionalism within both parties. The DDP lacked clear leadership and its generally academic and professional membership descended into internal and often abstract bickering over policy. The DVP too was divided between its business and non-commercial supporters, and despite Stresemann's efforts this remained a continuous source of conflict. It is not really surprising therefore that moves to bring about some kind of united liberal party came to nothing and as a result the case for German liberalism proved increasingly difficult to present to the electorate with any degree of conviction.

Ironically, one optimistic feature of party politics came from the unexpected quarter of the DNVP. Since 1919 the DNVP had been implacably opposed in principle to the republic and had refused to participate in government (see page 100). In electoral terms it had enjoyed considerable success, gaining 103 seats in December 1924. However, as the republic began to stabilise in the wake of the 1923 crisis, it became increasingly clear that the DNVP's hopes for the restoration of a more authoritarian regime were diminishing and that blind opposition would achieve nothing. Some of the powerful vested interests within the ranks of the DNVP recognised that if they were to exert any influence on government policy, then the party had to be prepared to participate in government. Consequently, the DNVP twice opted to join a government coalition in 1925 and 1927. This more accommodating policy towards the republic was an encouraging development. However, it was not popular with all elements of the party and when the DNVP vote fell by a quarter in the 1928 election, the more reactionary elements were able to reassert themselves and elect Hugenberg as the new leader. Hugenberg was a nationalist of the Pan-German kind, who utterly rejected the very concept of a parliamentary republic. He was also Germany's greatest media tycoon and owned 150 newspapers and a publishing house, as well as the world famous UFA film organisation. He now used all his resources to promote his political message. The DNVP reverted to a programme of unrestrained opposition to the republic and non-involvement in government. A year later it was working closely with the Nazis against the Young Plan (see page 125).

One of the factors contributing to the temporary phenomenon of nationalist moderation was the election of Field Marshal Hindenburg as president in 1925 - a development which has been interpreted in a number of different ways. On the one hand, his assumption of power did not immediately result in a marked swing to the right. Hindenburg proved to be absolutely loyal to his constitutional responsibilities and he carried out his presidential duties with absolute correctness. Those nationalists who had hoped that his election might facilitate a monarchist restoration or the creation of a more militaristic authoritarian regime were to be greatly disappointed. Indeed, it has been argued that with Hindenburg holding the presidential seals of office, Germany had at last found its true *Ersatzkaiser* and thereby the republic at last attained respectability. On the other hand, it is difficult to ignore the potential pitfalls of the appointment of an old man who in his heart felt no real identity with the republic and its values. His entourage was made up of mainly anti-republican figures, especially from the army, and he preferred to include the DNVP in government and to exclude the SPD if at all possible. In this sense, Hindenburg's view from the start was that 'government should move to the right' (Kolb). It was only after 1929 that the serious implications of this for Weimar democracy became fully apparent. As one historian has aptly put it: 'he refused to betray the republic, but he did not rally the people to its banner' (Nicholls).

It is difficult to escape the conclusion that the parliamentary and party system had failed to make any real progress in this middle period. It had merely coped. It had carried out the functions of government, but its successes can only be measured in relatively limited terms. There was no *putsch* from left or right. The anti-republican extremists were electorally contained. Law and order was restored and the activities of the various para-military groups severely curtailed. However, despite the good intentions of certain individuals and groups, there were no signs of any real strengthening or maturity in the political structure. Stable government just had not been established. This is not entirely surprising when, for example, one coalition government could fall over the issue of the national flag and another over the creation of denominational schools. Perhaps even more significant for the future was the growing cynicism which pervaded popular attitudes to party politics and the wheeler-dealing associated with the creation of most coalitions. This divorce between the people and 'the system' is most obviously revealed by the declining turn-out at elections (see table on page 140) and by the growing number of small fringe parties. In the final analysis the apparent stability of these years was simply a mirage. It deceived some people into believing that a genuine basis for political stabilisation had been achieved. It had not.

3 Gustav Stresemann and Weimar Foreign Policy

a) The Context

Weimar foreign policy was dominated by an unrelenting determination to revise the Treaty of Versailles. On no other issue was there such unanimity as in the desire to erase the 'shameful peace'. However, if there was agreement on the fundamental aim of German foreign policy a clear division of opinion existed over the means to that end. Those who might be termed 'the hardliners' believed that the implementation of the treaty's terms must be resisted wherever possible: reparations were not to be paid; disarmament flouted; and the territorial clauses rejected and overturned. They accepted that military conflict with France and its allies was almost unavoidable and that therefore Germany needed to be in a state of military preparedness. Typical of such views was Colonel Stülpnagel's memorandum which was sent to the Foreign Office in 1926 with the approval of Seeckt:

The immediate aim of German policy must be the regaining of full
1 sovereignty over the area retained by Germany, the firm acquisition of those areas at present separated from her, and the re-acquisition of those areas essential to the German economy. That is to say:
5 1. The liberation of the Rhineland and the Saar area.
2. The abolition of the Corridor and the regaining of Polish Upper Silesia.
3. The *Anschluss* of German Austria.
4. The abolition of the Demilitarised Zone.
10 These immediate political aims will produce conflict primarily with France and Belgium and with Poland which is dependent on them, then with Czechoslovakia and finally also with Italy ...
The above exposition of Germany's political aims ... clearly shows that the problem for Germany in the next stages of her political

15 development can only be the re-establishment of her position in
Europe, and that the regaining of her world position will be a task
for the distant future. Re-establishing a European position is for
Germany a question in which land forces will almost exclusively be
20 decisive, for the opponent of this resurrection is in the first place
France. It is certainly to be assumed that a reborn Germany will
eventually come into conflict with the American-English powers in
the struggle for raw materials and markets, and that she will then
need adequate maritime forces. But this conflict will be fought out
25 on the basis of a firm European position, after a new solution to the
Franco-German problem has been achieved through either peace
or war.

However, the moderate revisionists recognised that the dangerously
weak domestic position of Germany acted as a major constraint in the
pursuit of foreign policy. For this reason they believed that Germany
must follow a dual policy of economic development at home and
reconciliation abroad: only by working with the Allies could Germany
hope to alleviate the mill-stone of reparations which was holding back
the German economy; and only by restoring Germany's economic
strength could Germany hope to regain an influential voice in
international affairs. This policy of moderate revisionism came to be
known as 'fulfilment' and is most closely associated with the names of
Josef Wirth, chancellor May 1921-November 1922, and Gustav
Stresemann chancellor August-November 1923 and thereafter foreign
minister until his death in October 1929.

Wirth's adoption of the 'fulfilment' policy was extremely unpopular
in right-wing nationalist circles and there is little doubt that its
supporters became a particular target in the political violence of the early
1920s. Of course, popular backing for the policy was not really helped by
the developing inflationary crisis which many Germans simply put down
to the burden of reparations. Moreover, there was little sympathy from
the Allies, since actual reparations payments remained so limited. In this
sense 'fulfilment' without substantive fiscal and currency reform proved
to be a failure. Wirth's resignation at the end of 1922 resulted in the
hard-liners assuming control of Weimar foreign policy.

One further significance of Wirth's period of office was the signing of
the Soviet-German Treaty of Rapallo in April 1922. This was not an
alliance, but a treaty of friendship establishing full diplomatic relations
between the two countries. In addition, it was agreed to renounce all
claims for war damage and reparations; and to develop military
collaboration. Allied opinion at the time was horrified by this 'unholy
alliance', which was perceived as a German-led conspiracy against the
Versailles settlement. And it is certainly true that hardline revisionists in
the army and the Foreign Office supported a pro-Soviet strategy in the
belief that Russo-German friendship would undermine the need for

'fulfilment' with the Allies and could result in combined military action against Poland and the downfall of the entire Versailles settlement. However, those historians who have focused on such motives as guiding German foreign policy have tended to play up the significance of the hardliners at the expense of the key figures such as Wirth and Rathenau, who saw the Rapallo Treaty as part of a broader strategy. Certainly, they wanted Germany to escape from the isolation of the post-war years and they wanted to counter-balance the French hegemony on the continent. But equally, they never intended that the Rapallo Treaty should be pursued in isolation and at the expense of 'fulfilment'. They viewed Rapallo in the east as going hand in hand with 'fulfilment' in the west.

In the short-term, Wirth's foreign policy strategy brought only limited success. During the débacle of 1923 foreign policy was controlled by the hardliners who initiated a nationalistic policy of 'passive resistance'. However, though such a policy may have briefly satisfied certain nationalistic whims, the limitations of such an approach were soon clearly highlighted by the events of 1923. The reparations problem was not actually solved and Germany descended into hyper-inflation. Those German diplomats and politicians who had hoped to be able to make a stand against the Allies and Versailles only succeeded in underlining Germany's military and diplomatic weakness (which even friendship with the USSR could not disguise). At the height of the crisis in August 1923 Stresemann was appointed chancellor and the policy of 'fulfilment' was restored.

b) Stresemann's Formative Years

The development of Gustav Stresemann (1878-1929) into Weimar's one and only real statesman has long been the focus of controversy. Analysis of both his character and political philosophy has generated a wide range of interpretations. He has been categorised as both a fanatical nationalist and a 'great European' working for international reconciliation. He has been praised for his staunch support of parliamentary government and also condemned for being a charlatan democrat. He has been portrayed as a cynical opportunist and as a political idealist.

To some extent these contradictory opinions have arisen as the range of documentary sources has increased and as the historical perspective from which his career and his achievements have been viewed has changed. Thus in the wake of his early death, most assessments of Stresemann were favourable. However, after 1933 his reputation was blackened by Nazi historiography, whilst in western Europe the publication of some private letters first raised doubts about the sincerity of his foreign policy. The horrific legacy of the Third Reich and the first steps towards European co-operation provided the context for further reassessment, as German historians in particular sought to portray him as a prophet of European unity who stood in sharp relief to the proponents of German expansionism. Such a view became increasingly untenable after the publication of all his private papers and diaries and the opening up of the German Foreign Office files in the 1950s. Thereafter, interpretations have tended to depict him as the hard-headed German nationalist with a subtle grasp of power politics.

However, the wide range of interpretations has also come about simply because of the chequered nature of Stresemann's political career. Before 1921-2 there was little to suggest that Stresemann was to become the mainstay of a democratic republic. He graduated from Berlin University in Political Economy and then became a successful businessman. Politically, he was a child of the two great political ideals of nineteenth-century Germany - nationalism and liberalism - and in 1907 he became the youngest member of the *Reichstag* when he was elected as a National Liberal. In the years before 1914 his nationalism found expression in his support for Bülow's *Weltpolitik* and his membership of the Navy League. During the First World War it assumed even more extremist proportions: Stresemann was an ardent annexationist and supporter of the *Siegfriede* (see page 69); he campaigned for unrestricted submarine warfare; he opposed the 'peace resolution' and then conspired to bring about the downfall of Bethmann. By 1918 his support for the OHL and its imposition of the Treaty of Brest-Litovsk on Russia had earned him the title of 'Ludendorff's young man'. As a result, in 1919 after the break-up of the National Liberals he was deliberately excluded from the DDP and was left no real option but to form his own party, the DVP, which at first was hostile to the revolution and the republic and desired a restoration of the monarchy. Indeed, it was only in the wake of the failed Kapp Putsch and the murders of Erzberger and Rathenau that Stresemann led his party into adopting a more accommodating stance towards the republic. This sudden transformation of Stresemann into a *Vernunftrepublikaner* ('a rational republican') has certainly provided plenty of evidence for those critics who have seen his acceptance of the republic as superficial. However, such a charge is not entirely fair. His career during the war years has tended to overshadow his strong opposition to the self-interest of the conservatives and his support for moves towards constitutional government in the years before 1914. Ideally, Stresemann would have liked a parliamentary constitutional monarchy. That was not to be. By 1922 he had become convinced that the republic and its constitution provided Germany with its only realistic chance against the dictatorship of either left or right. This was quite simply a realistic pragmatic assessment. It cannot really be claimed that it was a decision motivated by a cynical desire to court popularity and to gain self-advancement.

c) Foreign Affairs, 1924-9

From its outset at the height of the 1923 crisis Stresemann's foreign policy was shaped by his realistic appreciation of the domestic and international situations. Unlike many nationalists he recognised that Germany had been militarily defeated and not simply 'stabbed in the back'; furthermore he rejected the simplistic solutions of those hardliners who failed to understand Germany's fundamental military weakness and who had brought the country to its knees in 1923. However, none of this is to deny that Stresemann's main aims were the liberation of Germany from the shackles of Versailles and its restoration as a 'great power' with equal status to Britain, France and America. Indeed, it has been said that the basic concept of Stresemann's foreign policy was derived from Germany's pre-1914 aspirations and his strategic methods evolved out of the post-1918 balance of power. In a private letter to the ex-Crown Prince in September 1927 Stresemann wrote:

1 In my opinion there are three great tasks that confront German foreign policy in the more immediate future: -
In the first place the solution of the Reparations question in a sense tolerable for Germany and the assurance of peace, which is an 5 essential premise for the recovery of our strength.
Secondly, the protection of Germans abroad, those 10 to 12 millions of our kindred who now live under a foreign yoke in foreign lands.
The third great task is the readjustment of our eastern frontiers; the 10 recovery of Danzig, the Polish corridor, and a correction of the frontier in Upper Silesia.
In the background stands the union with German Austria, although I am quite clear that this not merely brings no advantages to Germany, but seriously complicates the problem of the German 15 Reich ...
The question of a choice between east and west does not arise as the result of our joining the League. Such a choice can only be made when backed by military force. That, alas we do not possess.
We can neither become a continental spear-head for England, as 20 some believe, nor can we involve ourselves in an alliance with Russia. I would utter warning against any utopian ideas of coquetting with Bolshevism.

If offensive action was out of the question, Stresemann's only recourse was to diplomacy. But how could he achieve his aims in the context of the 1920s when, as he himself once remarked, he was only backed up by the power of German culture and the German economy? Firstly, he was prepared to recognise that France did have legitimate security interests and that as France also controlled the balance of power on the continent, a Franco-German rapprochement was an essential pre-requisite to solving outstanding problems. Secondly, he played on

Germany's vital importance to world trade in order to earn the goodwill and co-operation of Britain and the USA, both of whom were able to exert influence on French foreign policy. The sympathy of the USA was also vital in order to attract American capital into the German economy. Thirdly, so as to offset the diplomatic offensive in the west, he wished to maintain the Rapallo 'connection' with the USSR. However, he rejected out of hand those hardliners who desired an alliance with the communist power as the 'maddest of foreign policy makers'. Stresemann's strategy was therefore clearly in the tradition of Wirth's fulfilment. He was a moderate revisionist. In the long-term he wanted Germany to be the leading power in Europe once again. To that end co-operation and peace, particularly with the western powers, were in the best interests of Germany, even if this in practice limited his scope for change in the short-term.

The starting point of Stresemann's foreign policy was the thorny issue of reparations. As chancellor he had called off 'passive resistance' and agreed to resume the payment of reparations. The result of this was the Anglo-American Dawes Plan. Although the plan left the actual sum to be paid unchanged, it re-scheduled the monthly instalments over the first five years according to Germany's capacity to pay. Furthermore, it provided for a large loan to Germany to aid economic recovery. The

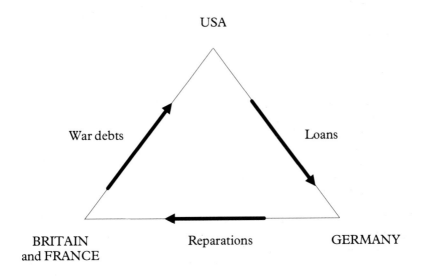

Reparations, War debts and Loans

Dawes Plan has been described as 'a victory for financial realism' and it was accepted by all interested parties in July 1924. For Stresemann its advantages were manifold: for the first time it clearly implied an international recognition of Germany's financial problems; it procured credit by means of the loan and subsequent investments for the cash-starved German economy; and it resulted in a French promise to evacuate the Ruhr during 1925. In the short-term the Dawes Plan was a success. The German economy was in actual fact not weakened, since it imported twice as much capital as was paid out in reparations. And the mere fact that reparations were being regularly paid certainly contributed to the Franco-German rapprochement of these years. However, it is now apparent that the whole system of international finance was precariously balanced upon the continued circulation of American loans, German reparations and Allied war debts. In attempting to break out of the politico-economic crisis of 1923 Stresemann had unwittingly linked Germany's fortunes to powerful external forces which were to exert enormous pressures after 1929.

The ending of the Ruhr crisis and the introduction of the Dawes Plan showed that the two sides could at least take each other's interests seriously. However, Stresemann continued to fear that Anglo-French friendship could lead to an alliance, especially if France began to feel threatened by Germany's industrial recovery. In order to pre-empt such a development Stresemann proposed in early 1925 a security pact for Germany's western frontiers, and although France was at first hesitant Britain and the USA both backed the initiative. The idea formed the basis for the Locarno treaties signed in October 1925. By the treaty of mutual guarantee Germany, France and Belgium agreed to respect their existing frontiers (including the demilitarised Rhineland) whilst Britain and Italy assumed the role of guarantors. By the treaties of arbitration Germany, Poland and Czechoslovakia simply agreed to settle future disputes peacefully, but there was no acceptance of the existing frontiers. The Locarno treaties represented the vital diplomatic development in the decade after 1919. Germany was liberated from its diplomatic isolation by the Allies and was again treated as an equal partner. In strategic terms Stresemann had also achieved a great deal at Locarno at very little cost. He had confirmed the status quo in the west, since Germany was in no position to alter the situation anyway, but in so doing he had also curtailed France's freedom of action - the occupation of the Ruhr or the annexation of the Rhineland were no longer a legitimate options. Moreover, by establishing a solid basis for Franco-German understanding Stresemann had lessened French interest in her allies in eastern Europe. The Poles certainly viewed the treaties as a major setback, since Stresemann had deliberately refused to confirm the frontiers in the east whilst conceding to French concerns about security in the west. In this sense Stresemann envisaged that Locarno would be followed by further advances; the early restoration of full German sovereignty over the Saar and the Rhineland or a reduction in reparations; and then later perhaps a revision of the eastern frontier. In the years immediately after Locarno there was indeed further diplomatic progress. Germany joined the League of Nations as a permanent member of the Council in 1926 and two years later it subscribed to the Kellogg-Briand Pact which was an international declaration outlawing 'war as an instrument of national policy'. Finally, in 1929 the Allies agreed to evacuate the Rhineland earlier than intended in return for a final settlement of the reparations issue. The result was the Young Plan, a revised scheme of payments by which Germany agreed to pay reparations until 1988, but the total sum was reduced to £1850 millions (only one-quarter of the figure demanded in 1921).

Although Stresemann viewed rapprochement with the west as his priority, he was also determined to remain on good terms with the USSR. As a result, the two countries signed the Treaty of Berlin in April 1926 in order to confirm the basis of the relationship established at Rapallo. This was not hypocrisy by Stresemann. It was simply a recognition that Germany's defence requirements because of its geographical position at the heart of Europe could never entirely be satisfied by either east or west. The Soviet relationship allayed strategic fears, opened up the possibility of a large commercial market, and placed even more pressure on Poland to satisfy German demands for frontier revision.

d) Assessment

In 1926 Stresemann was awarded, along with his British and French counterparts, the Nobel prize for peace. Only three years later at the age of 51 he died of a heart attack. The socialist newspaper *Vorwärts* wrote in its obituary column:

1 Stresemann's achievement was in line with the ideas of the international socialist movement. He saw that you can only serve your people by understanding other peoples. To serve collapsed Germany he set out on the path of understanding. He refused to
5 try to get back land which had gone forever. He offered our former enemies friendship. Being a practical man he saw that any other path would have left Germany without any hope of recovery. He covered the long distance from being a nationalist politician of conquest to being a champion of world peace. He fought with great
10 personal courage for the ideals in which he believed ... It is no wonder that right-wingers watched with horror as he went from his original camp to the opposite one. They could not accept him because doing so involved accepting that the Republic created by the workers had brought Germany from devastation to recovery.

There can be little doubt that Stresemann had achieved a great deal in a short space of time to transform both Germany's domestic and international positions. Moreover, the improvement had been achieved by conciliatory and peaceful methods. When one also considers the dire situation inherited in 1923 and the forces (both internal and external) stacked against him, it is perhaps not surprising that his policy has been described by the leading German historian of the Weimar Republic as 'astonishingly successful' (Kolb). However, it should be borne in mind that circumstances worked strongly in Stresemann's favour as well - from 1924 to 1929 the international context and the aura of economic prosperity were also vital factors in the shaping of events. Stresemann has also been criticised for over-estimating the revisionist potential of his rapprochement policy. And certainly, he himself became increasingly disappointed by the limits and slow pace of revision. By the time of his death the nationalist opposition was mobilising itself against the Young Plan and there was a growing sentiment that Stresemann's conciliation policy was coming to a dead end. It must be questioned therefore whether fundamental revision, particularly with regard to the Polish frontier, could ever have been achieved by Stresemann. As it was, his death and the onset of the world depression were followed by the collapse of the republic. In the years after 1929 gradualist revisionism gave way to a harder line, which later culminated in the aggressive revisionism and expansionism of the Third Reich. The distinction is an important one. For whatever the limitations and ambiguities of Stresemann's policy, his vision of Germany as a great power was founded upon the concepts of international peace and negotiated settlements. Like his political forebear, Bismarck, Stresemann recognised the importance of peace for Germany in the realm of international affairs. His achievement was indeed considerable - though by 1929 his policy had not lasted long enough or gone far enough to establish a momentum that could survive the very different circumstances of the 1930s.

4 How Stable was the Weimar Republic in the Years 1924-9?

The years 1924-9 undoubtedly mark the high point of the Weimar Republic. By comparison with the periods of crisis before and after 1924-9 these years do appear stable. The very real increase in prosperity experienced by many and the cultural vitality of the period both give some credence to the cliché of 'the golden twenties'. However, historians have generally tended to emphasise the relative nature of this stability. Kolb describes these years as ones of 'relative stabilisation' and Peukert writes of 'deceptive stability'. This is because the stability was in actual fact strictly limited in scope.

The economic recovery was built on unstable foundations and created a false image of prosperity. Structural problems persisted in the economy and they were only masked by an increasing reliance on credit from abroad. In this way Germany's future economic stability became inextricably tied to powerful external forces over which it had no control. Hindsight, therefore, now allows historians to see that in the late twenties any disruption to the world's trading pattern or its financial markets was bound to have a particularly destabilising effect on an already precarious German economy. German society too was still riven by deep class antagonisms (as well as by important regional and denominational differences) which inhibited the development of any real national consensus. The war and the years of crisis had left a residue of bitterness, fear and resentment between capital and labour. Following the introduction of the state arbitration scheme in 1924, its procedure

Retter Stresemann

Mai 1923

„Er schaut nach rechts, er schaut nach links — er wird mich retten!"

Der Retter Stresemann - *The Saviour Stresemann*

was invoked almost as a matter of course when the intention had been that its use would be the exception not the rule. As a result 76,000 industrial disputes were assessed between 1924 and 1932! And in 1928 a massive lock-out occurred in the Ruhr ironworks when the employers refused to accept the arbitration award. It was the most serious industrial confrontation of the Weimar period and underlines the bitterness of industrial relations even before the onset the world depression. The lack of consensus was also reflected in the political sphere where the parliamentary system had failed to build on the revolutionary changes of 1918. There was no effective consolidation nor any significant sign of political maturation - in particular, the main democratic parties had still not recognised the vital necessity of working together in a spirit of compromise. There is also strong evidence to suggest that even before the political crisis of 1930-3 Weimar was losing its claim to political legitimacy in the minds of many Germans, especially the middle classes. In this sense it was not so much the theoretical weaknesses of the constitution or the existence of a multi-party system and short-lived coalitions which were the fundamental political problems, but the failure in this period to establish a widely-respected political culture which could withstand a future crisis. Even the successes of Stresemann in the field of foreign affairs have to be offset by the fact that significant numbers of his fellow countrymen at the time rejected his policy out of hand and pressed for a more hardline approach.

In reality, the middle years of the Weimar Republic were only stable relative to the periods before and after. The actual condition of the economy, the lack of political maturity and the depth of social divisions suggest that the fundamental problems inherited from the war and the years of crisis had not been resolved. They persisted and to some extent were exacerbated and thus, when renewed crisis set in during 1929-30, the Weimar system did not prove itself strong enough to withstand the storm.

Making notes on 'Weimar: Relative Stability'

The key-word in this chapter, as you have probably realised by now, is 'stability'. Your notes must therefore be geared towards you consciously trying to get clear in your own mind the degree of stability achieved during this period. There is also quite a lot of detail. Be careful! You must not write down details for their own sake, but as the supporting evidence for the main ideas and arguments. The following headings and guidelines should help you to achieve these aims.

1. The Economy. Summarise in your own words the arguments of Borchardt and Holtfrerich. Now re-read this section and note down the details which support each side. You should then be in a position

to write your own brief concluding analysis about Weimar's economic condition. Was it: 'terminally sick'? 'a false prosperity'? 'temporarily off the rails'?

2. Domestic Politics. Draw up a list of strengths and weaknesses of the Weimar political system in this period. How substantial was Weimar's political recovery?

3. Foreign Policy.
   3.1 The post-war context.
   3.2 Stresemann's background. Compile a timeline of Stresemann's life and career up to 1923. Then write a brief political character sketch focusing on what you consider to have been the major influences on him.
   3.3 Foreign affairs, 1924-9. Explain how and why each one of the various developments in Germany's foreign policy:
      a) contributed to international reconciliation
      b) improved Germany's international position
      c) was opposed by Stresemann's opponents.
   3.4 Assessment. Have Stresemann's achievements been exaggerated?

4. How stable was Weimar in the years 1924-9? What is the opinion of the author on this question? Do you agree with him or do you think he is too pessimistic?

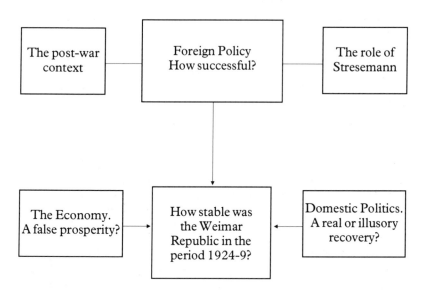

Summary - Weimar: Relative Stability, 1924-9

Source-based questions on 'Weimar: Relative Stability'

1 The German Economy in the late 1920s
Read carefully the reports of the Deutsche Bank on pages 112-3 and the report of G. Parker on page 111. Answer the following questions.
a) Explain the following references: 'over-high social payments'; 'the Experts' Plan'. (2 marks)
b) Explain in your own words
   (i) the economic analysis of Deutsche Bank
   (ii) the economic analysis of Gilbert Parker (4 marks)
c) How do you explain the differences between the two reports? (4 marks)

2 The Aims of Weimar Foreign Policy
Read carefully the memorandum of Stülpnagel on pages 118-19 and the letter of Stresemann on page 122. Answer the following questions.
a) Compare and contrast the aims of German foreign policy as outlined in the two sources. (6 marks)
b) The first extract is a political memorandum from a leading army officer and the second is from a private letter by Stresemann. In what ways would this affect a historian's assessment of the extracts' reliability as evidence? (4 marks)
c) In the light of developments in the 1930s comment on Stülpnagel's statement in lines 19-25 'Re-establishing a European position ... adequate maritime forces'. (4 marks)

3 Gustav Stresemann
Read carefully the obituary of Stresemann on pages 125-6 and study the cartoon on page 127. Answer the following questions.
a) Comment on the claims in the *Vorwärts* obituary that
   (i) 'Stresemann's achievement was in line with the ideas of the international socialist movement', and
   (ii) 'the Republic created by the workers had brought Germany from devastation to recovery'. (4 marks)
b) What is the cartoonist trying to communicate about Stresemann? (the little boy is the German Michael - a stereotype for the stupid/naive German). (5 marks)
c) How reliable are these two sources as evidence of Stresemann's political reputation in Germany in the late 1920s? (4 marks)
d) To what extent do these sources and other evidence known to you support the assertion that Stresemann was Weimar's saviour? (7 marks)

CHAPTER 7

Weimar: the Final Years, 1929-33

In October 1929 the international shock-waves caused by the Wall Street Crash ushered in the world economic crisis. A little over three years later on 30 January 1933 Hitler was appointed chancellor and Germany descended into the tyrannical dictatorship of the Third Reich. However, it is very dangerous to posit too direct a causal link between these two events. As the crisis unfolded it became increasingly likely that liberal democracy would give way to some variant of authoritarian rule, but almost to the very last moment history could have taken a different course. Hitler's Nazi regime must not be viewed as an inevitable consequence of the Weimar's demise. This, therefore, raises two vital questions, which though intimately linked, are clearly separate. 'Why did Weimar democracy collapse?' and 'Why did the Nazis, and not some other political group, take power?'. It is the former question which is the real focus of this chapter and of this particular volume. For a fuller discussion of the rise of Hitler and National Socialism it will be necessary to consult the companion volume in this series, *Germany: The Third Reich, 1933-45.*

1 The Impact of the World Economic Crisis

There is no dispute amongst historians that the world economic crisis was an event of epoch-making significance. The crisis was felt throughout the world and it struck Germany in a particularly savage fashion. The really contentious issue is whether it should be considered as the direct cause of Weimar's collapse or merely the occasion.

Germany was probably more susceptible to the repercussions of the Wall Street Crash than any other country. Almost immediately the loans and investment dried up and this was soon followed by demands for the repayment of those loans which had been previously advanced so willingly. At the same time, the crisis precipitated a further decline in the prices of food and raw materials, as industrialised nations reduced their imports. But the knock-on effects of this action rebounded upon the more advanced economies, since many primary producers could no longer afford to import manufactured goods. World trade slumped as demand collapsed. In this situation German industry could no longer pay its way. Unsupported by loans and with diminished export markets, prices and wages fell whilst the number of bankruptcies increased. During the winter of 1929-30 unemployment rose above 2 million. Only 12 months after the Crash, it had reached 3 million. By September 1932 it stood at 5.1 million. It peaked in early 1933, when 6.1 million Germans were unemployed.

Yet, on their own such figures can only provide a limited understanding of an event like the depression. The unemployment figures, for example, do not take into account those who never registered. Nor do they recognise the extent of short-time working throughout German industry. Above all, such statistics fail to convey the extent of the sociological and psychological consequences of this disaster. For the depression in Germany was all pervasive; few families escaped its detrimental effects. Many manual workers, both skilled and unskilled, faced the prospect of indefinite unemployment. For their wives there was the impossible task of trying to feed families and keep homes warm on the money provided by limited social security benefits. However, such problems were not limited to the working class: the depression also dragged down the middle classes. From the small-scale shopkeepers to the graduate professionals in law and medicine, people struggled to survive in a world where their goods and services were decreasingly in demand. For such casualties the decline in their economic position was further accentuated by the loss of pride and respectability, which accompanied poverty and unemployment. In the countryside the situation was no better than in the towns. As world demand contracted further, the agricultural depression deepened markedly, leading to widespread rural poverty. For some tenant farmers there was even the ultimate ignominy of eviction from tenancies which had been in their families for generations.

In the relative prosperity of today it is difficult to appreciate the scale of the economic and social suffering which struck Germany in the early 1930s. To many ordinary respectable Germans it must have seemed as if society itself was breaking down uncontrollably. One-third of the population was on the dole; the city of Cologne could not pay the interest on its debts; banks closed their doors; and in Berlin large crowds of unemployed youngsters were kept occupied with open-air games of chess and cards! In such a situation it is perhaps not surprising that people lost faith in the Weimar Republic and saw salvation in the solutions offered by political extremism.

However, it is important that this atmosphere of catastrophe is put into some kind of analytical context. It has already been established that the Weimar economy, even during its period of 'relative stabilisation', faced many fundamental problems. This therefore suggests that the world economic crisis should really be viewed as simply the final push (albeit an excessively hefty one) which brought the Weimar system crashing down. Comparisons with other industrialised nations also suggest that a monocausal focus on the world economic crisis is over-simplistic. The economic and social impact of the depression in Germany was certainly more severe than in either Britain or France, but it was on a par with the American experience. In Germany 1 in 3 workers were unemployed in 1933 and industrial production by 1932 had fallen by 42 per cent of its 1929 level - in the USA the comparable figures were 1 in 4 and 46 per cent. Despite such similarities the USA was never confronted by the possibility of a wholesale collapse of the political system. On the other hand in Germany the economic crisis quickly became a political crisis simply because there was a latent lack of confidence in the system which fundamentally weakened its political legitimacy in its hour of need. Taken together these two points suggest that the Great Depression certainly accelerated the end of the Weimar Republic, but only because its prevailing economic circumstances were already dire and its democratic foundations were so poorly established.

2 Chancellor Brüning, 1930-2

a) The Advent of Presidential Government

In 1929 the German government was Hermann Müller's Grand Coalition, which had been formed after the general election of 1928. Despite being supported by a majority in the *Reichstag,* Müller's government had from the start been subject to severe internal divisions which were exacerbated further by the drift to the right of the Centre Party and the death of Stresemann. Not surprisingly in the context of the time, it was an issue of government finance which finally brought down the government in March 1930. The sharp increase in unemployment had created a large deficit in the insurance scheme, and the SPD and the DVP could not reconcile their differences on how to tackle it. The SPD, as the political representatives of the trade unions, wanted to increase the contributions and to maintain the levels of welfare payments. The DVP, on the other hand, had strong ties with big business. It insisted on reducing benefits in order to cut costs and to balance the budget. In this situation Müller resigned as chancellor and was replaced by Heinrich Brüning, the parliamentary leader of the Centre Party.

Brüning's response to the growing economic crisis was to propose increased taxes and substantial cuts in government expenditure, but his budget was rejected in the *Reichstag* in July 1930. In this situation Brüning put the proposals into effect by means of an emergency decree signed by the president according to Article 48. The *Reichstag* challenged the legality of this action and voted for the withdrawal of the decree. Deadlock had been reached. Brüning therefore asked Hindenburg to dissolve the *Reichstag* and to call an election for September 1930. He was hopeful that in the developing crisis the electorate would be encouraged to back his centre-right coalition. However, the election results proved him to be disastrously wrong (see the table on page 140). The real beneficiaries were the Nazis who achieved electoral breakthrough and suddenly became the second largest party in the *Reichstag* with 107 seats. Brüning's parliamentary position was now even more difficult and he could only carry on as chancellor because he retained the support of Hindenburg and because the SPD decided to 'tolerate' his use of Article 48 so as to preserve the republic from the extremists.

Over the years Brüning's appointment as chancellor has proved to be highly controversial, though the points of interest have shifted over time. Initially, the debate revolved around the political question of Brüning's aims and the nature of his government. Some historians saw him as essentially a sincere statesman desperately struggling in the face of enormous difficulties 'to save democracy'. They believed that his recourse to presidential government by the use of Article 48 was an understandable reaction to the inadequacies of party government in the crisis and that the real hammer-blow for German democracy came with his dismissal in 1932 rather than with his appointment two years earlier. Others portrayed him as a conservative reactionary, opposed to democracy, who arbitrarily used the emergency powers which consequently paved the way for Hitler's dictatorship. In their view Brüning's chancellorship not only marked the first vital step on the road to the dissolution of the republic, but also made possible Hitler's subsequent dictatorship.

On the whole, the original defenders of Brüning's political stance were forced to give way as further evidence became available. Most damning of all, ironically, was the publication after Brüning's death in 1970 of his own *Memoirs, 1918-34*. This established beyond any reasonable doubt that he was an arch-conservative and monarchist who had little sympathy for the democratic republic. He stated that his aims in government were decisively to weaken the *Reichstag* and to re-establish a Bismarckian-type constitution with a more powerful executive which could ignore the power and influence of the political left. To these ends he was prepared to use the emergency powers of the presidency and to look for backing from the traditional elites of German society.

Therefore, it is now generally accepted that Brüning's appointment did mark a decisive move away from proper parliamentary government. The office of chancellor (as well as the presidency) was in the hands of someone unsympathetic to democracy and from September 1930 Brüning's political miscalculation resulted in a decisive weakening of the *Reichstag* and the emergence of the Nazis as a national political force. It must also be borne in mind that Brüning had been manoeuvred into office by a select circle of political intriguers who surrounded the ageing president - Otto Meissner, the president's state secretary, Oskar von Hindenburg, the president's son, and Major General Kurt von Schleicher, the political voice of the army. They too had lost faith in the democratic process and they saw in Brüning a respectable conservative figure, who could front an authoritarian government backed by the army.

b) Coping with the Depression

If nothing else, Brüning's economic policy was at least consistent.

Throughout his two years in office he pursued a strong deflationary programme in an attempt to balance the budget: government spending was drastically cut and taxes raised with the result that the 'squeeze' massively increased the numbers of unemployed. After 1945 Brüning was roundly condemned by most economists and historians as at best naive and weak and at worst grossly incompetent. It was generally believed in the post-war economic consensus based upon Keynesian ideas of deficit financing that government needed to pursue an expansionist reflationary policy in order to counter the effects of depression. By sticking to a policy of retrenchment, it was generally believed, Brüning had seriously exacerbated the economic and social situation and consequently facilitated the rise of the Nazis.

It is often stated that a historian is a product of his own epoch. Perhaps, then, we should not be surprised that in the mid-1970s when the world once again moved into recession after a quarter-century of growth and when doubts arose about the validity of Keynesian principles that an economic historian, Borchardt, began to re-interpret Brüning's reputation in a much more sympathetic fashion. Borchardt's work has already been alluded to in the discussion of Weimar's economy in its middle period (see page 113). Indeed, Borchardt's assessment of Weimar at that time as 'abnormal' and incurably 'sick' forms an important part of his revisionist assessment of Brüning's economic strategy.

In simple terms, Borchardt claims that Brüning had no real room for manoeuvre in his economic policy and that as a result there was no feasible alternative to stringent deflation - reflation by deficit financing was just not a viable option. This was partly because of the legacy from the 1920s which meant that the German economy entered the depression with severe structural weaknesses, in particular, excessively high and uncompetitive wage levels and already large government deficits. But it was also because of the practical restrictions limiting any kind of economic expansion. Such an approach would have required either credit from abroad, which would have been linked to strict pre-conditions, or an increase in the money supply from the *Reichsbank,* which not only would have resurrected fears of inflation, but would have also contravened the legal terms of the bank's operations according to the recently agreed Young Plan. Finally, Borchardt contends that even if the financial means had been available, the real extent of the depression was only recognised in the summer of 1931 and by that time it was already too late to implement measures to prevent unemployment rising above six million. In this sense Borchardt sees Brüning as a relatively innocent pawn at the mercy of remorseless economic forces.

Borchardt's thesis has proved to be highly contentious since it has decisively challenged certain well-established assumptions. Leading the opposition to Borchardt has been Holtfrerich who continues to claim that there were clear policy alternatives, but no real determination to apply them. He accepts that there were weaknesses in Weimar's economy during the middle years, but he rejects the idea of a 'sick' economy doomed to collapse even before the depression (see page 113). In Holtfrerich's opinion Brüning remained wedded to his economic strategy, despite suggestions to the contrary from within his own government, primarily because of his objectives in the fields of domestic politics and foreign affairs. In effect Brüning aimed to exploit the depression by maintaining the deflation strategy in order to demonstrate to the Allies that the payment of reparations was no longer financially possible, and also to discredit and decisively weaken the social and economic base upon which the republic was built. It was not so much that circumstances prevented Brüning from confronting the problems of the depression - rather it was simply that his priorities lay elsewhere and they took precedence.

The historiographical debate between Borchardt's and Holtfrerich's interpretations has proved to be particularly fierce and even now shows no real sign of resolution. Holtfrerich and his supporters have gone some way to suggest that Brüning did have at least some room for manoeuvre, even if it was not as much as was once believed. An alternative economic strategy in the summer of 1931, such as a work creation scheme in the construction industry and/or the reduction of agricultural subsidies to facilitate spending elsewhere, might just have been enough to mitigate the worst effects of the depression during 1932. That these were rejected on essentially political grounds because of Brüning's determination to show that Germany could not afford to pay reparations is also probably a correct assessment. However, Borchardt has succeeded in showing that there were no easy solutions to the economic crisis and that any reflation strategy would have had serious repercussions. Holtfrerich's carefully planned alternatives are proposed with all the facility provided by hindsight. Borchardt has effectively scotched the glib criticism of Brüning by many economic historians that the depression could simply have been tackled by a good dose of deficit financing, especially at a time when it would have meant Germany acting in economic isolation from the rest of the world. He has also broadened the area of discussion beyond the narrow confines of 1929-32 and demonstrated without doubt the serious nature of Weimar's economic condition before the onset of the world depression. Borchardt's thesis is an attractive one and despite some valid criticisms he has significantly and decisively changed the focus of academic debate on this period of history. For that reason his defence of Brüning's economic policy is on balance the more convincing, if not yet finally proven.

c) Brüning's Fall from Power

In the spring of 1932 Hindenburg's first seven-year term of office as president came to an end. Brüning committed himself to securing the old man's re-election and despite the very effective campaign fought by the Nazis on behalf of Hitler, it was Hindenburg who won on the second ballot with 19.3 million votes (53 per cent) against Hitler's 13.4 million (36.8 per cent). However, Hindenburg showed no gratitude to Brüning and at the end of May 1932 the president forced his chancellor's resignation by refusing to sign any more emergency decrees. Why was this?

The immediate cause was the president's displeasure at Brüning's latest economic proposal to deploy 600,000 unemployed workers on *Junker* estates in East Prussia. Such a plan was portrayed as 'agrarian bolshevism' in landowning circles and it alienated Brüning from Germany's social elite. However, this was simply the occasion rather than the real cause of Brüning's fall.

By the end of 1931 popular confidence in Brüning had begun to wane as the effects of the depression and the deflation strategy continued to take their toll. In June Germany was caught up in the banking crash and one of its major institutions, the Danat, closed its doors to customers. By the end of the year unemployment was approaching five million and increasingly political tensions were being played out in the streets. Doubts about Brüning were also beginning to emerge among the clique surrounding President Hindenburg, as General Groener, the defence minister, later reflected:

1 I knew very well that the intention was to bring down the Chancellor. In the course of the winter, the Reich President had twice mentioned to me that Dr. Brüning did not quite represent his ideal as Reich Chancellor. He did not accept my comment that at
5 the moment he would not find a better one. General von Schleicher had also made no bones about the fact that he was thinking in terms of a change of Chancellor. In view of his connexions with the Reich President's entourage, it can be assumed that he took part in the removal of Dr. Brüning as
10 Chancellor. During the absence of the Reich President in Neudeck, his country estate, where Brüning's fall was decided upon, General von Schleicher was in continual contact by telephone with Hindenburg's son.

It is, therefore, now generally agreed that Brüning's fall from power had been prompted by the group surrounding the old man. Schleicher, recognising Brüning's limitations and unpopularity, had become convinced that the Nazis could no longer be ignored and must be included as the populist element of a more right-wing government which did not rely on the 'toleration' of the Social Democrats. It is quite clear from Goebbels' diaries that weeks before Brüning's eventual resignation intrigue and rumour were already rife:

8 May 1932

1 ... The *Führer* has an important interview with Schleicher in the presence of a few gentlemen of the President's immediate circle. All goes well. The *Führer* has spoken decisively. Brüning's fall is expected shortly. The President of the Reich will withdraw his 5 confidence from him. The plan is to constitute a Presidential Cabinet. The *Reichstag* will be dissolved. Repressive enactments are to be cancelled. We shall be free to go ahead as we like, and mean to outdo ourselves in propaganda.

10 11 May 1932

The *Reichstag* drags on. Groener's position is shaken; the army no longer supports him. Even those with most to do with him urge his downfall.

... Brüning is trying to salvage what he can. He speaks in the 15 *Reichstag* and cleverly beats a retreat on foreign politics. There he becomes aggressive. He believes himself within sight of the goal. He does not mention Groener at all. So he too has given him up! The whole debate turns on the lifting of the ban on the SA. Groener strongly objects to this. It will be his undoing.

20 24 May 1932

... Saturday will see the end of Brüning. Secretary of State Meissner leaves for Neudeck. Now we must hope for the best. The list of ministers is more or less settled: von Papen, Chancellor; von Neurath, Foreign Minister, and then a list of unfamiliar names. 25 The main point as far as we are concerned is to ensure that the *Reichstag* is dissolved ...

30 May 1932

The bomb has exploded. Brüning has presented the resignation of his entire Cabinet ... The system has begun to crumble ... Meet the 30 *Führer* at Nauen. The President wished to see him in the course of the afternoon ... The conference with the President went off well. The SA prohibition is going to be cancelled. Uniforms are to be allowed again. The *Reichstag* is to be dissolved.

If one accepts the explanation of Brüning's fall having been engineered at an appropriate moment by the long-standing intrigue of a presidential clique, one might be tempted to view Brüning as an innocent political sacrifice - as he himself did in his *Memoirs*. However, it should also be borne in mind that Brüning was in the end a victim of a political situation pre-dating the winter of 1931-2 which he himself had lived with since 1930. Certainly, he was ousted by the president without reference to the *Reichstag,* but until that moment Brüning had only survived as chancellor because he enjoyed the backing of the president. Brüning had concurred with the creation of presidential government and in such a political environment it is hard to defend him when he later proved to be an amateur in the faction and intrigue of the presidential court.

d) Assessment

Although most certainly not a democrat, Brüning was an honest, hard-working and honourable man with a deep sense of patriotism and an earnest desire to extricate his country from its crisis. His aims were: firstly, to end the payment of reparations and to accelerate the revision of the Versailles treaty; and secondly, to strengthen the executive at the expense of the *Reichstag* and in the long run to create an authoritarian regime. In many respects Brüning was making good progress according to these criteria when he was dismissed (reparations were eventually abolished by the Lausanne Conference in June 1932). However, he was not astute enough to recognise how dangerous and unstable the politico-economic crisis had become in Germany by 1932 and how precarious was his own position. Whilst Brüning retained the confidence of the president he was insulated by the screen of presidential government from the political realities. He thus proved incapable of giving the nation at large any sense of leadership in its hour of need. With no real hope of improvement, it is not surprising that large sections of the population became radicalised and looked towards the Nazis. Brüning himself certainly had no truck with Nazism and he continued to uphold the rule of law, but his brand of moderate authoritarianism reasserted the influence of the old elites at the heart of government and accustomed the public to rule by decree. In this way democracy was significantly undermined and the way was cleared for more extreme political solutions later on.

In the end it is hard to escape the conclusion that Brüning's chancellorship was a dismal failure. However, the appalling economic conditions of the time and the unforeseen and tyrannical aftermath of the Nazi dictatorship enable that failure to be tempered by a degree of sympathy. Brüning's failure was a tragic one.

3 The Rise of National Socialism

Although it is not the task of this volume to explain why the Hitler dictatorship succeeded Weimar democracy in 1933, the rise of Nazism is a vital feature of the years 1929-33 and it must be considered as an integral factor in the decline of the republic. In particular, it must be explained why National Socialism emerged as a mass movement (in the *Reichstag* election of July 1932 it polled 37.4 per cent of the vote, see the table on page 140), when in the 1920s it had been no more than a fringe party at *Reichstag* elections. For, although Hitler did not come to power as a result of an election, it is undoubtedly true that his party's electoral strength represented a popular power base which in the end could not be ignored in the political manoeuvres in the last year of Weimar's existence.

Weimar *Reichstag* Election Results, 1919-32

	1919	1920	1924	1924	1928	1930	1932	1932
Total on register (in millions)	36.8	35.9	38.4	39.0	41.2	43.0	44.2	44.4
Size of poll (per cent)	83.0	79.2	74.4	78.8	75.6	82.0	84.1	80.6
Total no. of seats in *Reichstag*	423	459	472	493	491	577	608	584
NSDAP Seats	-	-	32	14	12	107	230	196
Per Cent	-	-	6.5	3.0	2.6	18.3	37.3	33.1
DNVP Seats	44	71	95	103	73	41	37	52
Per Cent	103	15.1	19.5	20.5	14.2	7.0	5.9	8.3
DVP Seats	19	65	45	51	45	30	7	11
Per Cent	4.4	13.9	9.2	10.1	8.7	4.5	1.2	1.9
ZP/BVP Seats	91	85	81	88	78	87	97	90
Per Cent	19.7	18.0	15.6	17.3	15.2	14.8	15.7	15.0
DDP Seats	75	39	28	32	25	20	4	2
Per Cent	18.5	8.3	5.7	6.3	4.9	3.8	1.0	1.0
SPD Seats	165	102	100	131	153	143	133	121
Per Cent	37.9	21.7	20.5	26.0	29.8	24.5	21.6	20.4
USPD Seats	22	84						
Per Cent	7.6	17.9						
KPD Seats	-	4	62	45	54	77	89	100
Per Cent	-	2.1	12.6	9.0	10.8	13.1	14.3	16.9
Others Seats	7	9	29	29	51	72	11	12
Per Cent	1.6	2.9	10.3	7.8	14.0	14.0	2.9	2.9

Nazi ideology was hardly original. Nor was it particularly different from the programme of a host of other right-wing groups in Germany in the early 1920s. It was in essence simply a mixture of strong German nationalism, and by extension imperialism (*Lebensraum*) and racism, with its virulent brand of anti-Semitism and its veneration of the superior Aryan master-race. Such ideas were not uncommon in the late nineteenth century. They were to be found in the cheap and vulgar pamphlets sold to the masses in the large cities as well as within the more respectable corridors of Germany's great universities. They had also formed the basis for the programme of influential pressure groups, such as the Pan-German League. As a political philosophy then Nazism lacked real intellectual depth. It was superficial and simplistic. It was not even a rational system of thought, for there were glaring contradictions, particularly between its militaristic imperialism and its backward-looking social policy. However, despite such weaknesses Nazism succeeded in associating itself more effectively than any other political group as the most powerful opposition to the republic. The scapegoats of Nazi politics - the Jews, the communists, the socialists, the liberals - were all identified directly with Weimar democracy and then ruthlessly exploited as being responsible for Germany's condition. Ideologically, Nazism established itself as the antithesis of the values and system of Weimar. Consequently, when Weimar entered upon its final crisis Nazi ideas appeared to have been vindicated.

By 1929 and the onset of Weimar's final crisis the Nazi Party itself was also in a much stronger position to take advantage of its status as the 'we told you so' party. Despite the ignominious failure of the Munich Putsch of 1923 (discussed in detail in *Germany: The Third Reich, 1933-45*), Hitler had used the years of relative stability to rebuild and restructure the party on the premise of securing power by means of a policy of legality. Most significant of all was the fundamental reorganisation of the party according to the principle of *Führer* power (*Führerprinzip*). Not only did this reduce internal differences and strengthen Hitler's own personal position, but it also resulted in the creation of a vertical party structure throughout Germany. By this system the responsibility for the party in a particular region was placed in the hands of a *Gauleiter* (regional party boss) who was answerable to Hitler alone. At the same time the Nazis recognised the importance of what has been termed 'associationism' - and so formal associations were penetrated or created in a deliberate attempt to counteract the established influence of alternative political 'cultures' such as socialism and Catholicism. 'Associated' organisations were created for teachers, students, doctors, craftsmen and a host of other social groups. The party also developed a clear and recognisable identity with its paraphernalia of flags, uniforms, salutes and insignia. Such a militaristic image found further expression in the ritualistic meetings and rallies when the psychological forces of 'mass suggestion' and 'regimentation' took effect. All these activities were supplemented by a tireless dynamism and a sophisticated grasp of new technology and communications for propaganda. As a result, by 1929 party membership stood at nearly 100,000 and most of the other right-wing racist groups in Germany had been swallowed up. The Nazis had created a sophisticated party machine geared to the demands of winning support in a mass democracy.

With the developments in information technology in the 1970s, research and analysis into who voted Nazi and the reasons why grew into a major theme of historical study. As a result, the traditional view of

National Socialism as a middle-class movement, 'the extremism of the centre' (Lipset), although still containing a fair degree of truth, is now considered to be too simplistic to be historically valid. Instead, it is now generally believed that the key feature of Nazi electoral support was its ability to appeal to all sections of German society. Unlike many other parties in Germany the Nazis were not constrained by regional, denominational and class ties, and were thus able to establish a broader cross-section of support. Thus by 1932 they were the only party who could claim to have a major presence in every region of the country. In short, the NSDAP became Germany's first genuine *Volkspartei* or broad-based people's party. However, the breadth of Nazi support should not hide the fact that certain social groups were more attracted to Nazism than others. In those areas where Catholicism predominated, the Nazi breakthrough was less marked, whereas the more Protestant regions were more likely to vote Nazi. Likewise, the Nazis fared less well in the large industrial cities, but gained greater support in the countryside and in the residential suburbs. These trends were probably the result of the ideological and organisational strengths of Catholicism and socialism which made it much harder for the Nazis to break down the traditional loyalties of working-class and Catholic communities. Their traditional 'associationism' was stronger, whereas the Protestants, the farmers and the middle classes were not so tied and were, therefore, perhaps more likely to accept the Nazi message.

Despite these variations National Socialism developed into a genuinely national mass movement, appealing to very different social groups. This tends to substantiate the view that it was able to project itself quite successfully in a variety of different guises. Nazism was new, modern and dynamic and at the same time traditional, conservative and reassuring; it was against both capitalism and socialism; above all it was both revolutionary and reactionary, since it wished to destroy the republic while at the same time promising a return to a glorious bygone age. This dualism was at the heart of Nazi electoral success. It was further reinforced by the deliberate cultivation by the Nazi propaganda machine of two other key ideas: firstly, the *Führer* cult in which Hitler was portrayed as a messiah-type figure sent to save Germany; and secondly the unifying theme of a *Volksgemeinschaft* (People's Community), which promised to create a genuine national community bridging class and social divisions. Consequently, when the world economic crisis struck the already weak and unstable political and economic structure of Weimar, National Socialism was ideally placed to benefit. And as it flourished, Weimar's chances of survival were progressively diminished.

4 The Final Months of the Republic

From Brüning's fall in May 1932 until Hitler's appointment in January

1933 Germany's destiny was increasingly decided by the intrigue of a few key personalities surrounding the president. This tendency had already been established under Brüning, but under chancellors Papen (May-December 1932) and Schleicher (December 1932-January 1933), it became even more marked. What were the aims of this conservative nationalist clique and why did they fail to achieve a political solution which could have pre-empted Hitler's accession to power?

Brüning himself had recognised that his presidential government was an inadequate long-term constitutional solution. He had actually considered the possibility of restoring the Hohenzollern monarchy in the form of Wilhelm II's son as a means of giving the regime both legitimacy and a degree of popular appeal to counter that of Nazism, but he received no real support from anyone else in the cabal. Papen headed a cabinet dominated by aristocratic landowners and industrialists, which soon earned the nickname of the 'cabinet of barons', looked towards the Italian fascist model of 'corporatism' to create a 'New State': a nationalist, authoritarian and an anti-parliamentarian regime run by the conservative elites. Yet, despite Papen's 'success' in abolishing the state government of Prussia on 20 July by simply declaring a state of emergency and appointing himself Reich Commissioner for Prussia, his constitutional plans showed no real grasp of political realities. In September his cabinet had suffered a massive vote of no confidence by 512 votes to 42. In his frustration he was proposing by the end of 1932 to implement a 'fighting programme' by using the army and police to dissolve parliament once and for all, to crush all political parties and to force through a new authoritarian constitution. Bearing in mind the degree of political violence between the rival para-military organisations by this time, the implementation of such a plan would have risked causing a civil war and Papen found himself without real support even from within the presidential circle.

The aim of Weimar's last chancellor, Schleicher, was what has been termed 'a policy of the diagonal'. This was an attempt to create a more broadly based government by splitting the Nazis and attracting the support of the more socialist wing of the NSDAP and by gaining some support from the trade unions with a programme of public works. In this way Schleicher intended to project himself as the chancellor of national reconciliation. However, his political manoeuvres came to nothing, whilst his gesture towards the trade unions had only created mistrust within the ranks of the traditional vested interests. In this situation Hindenburg finally agreed, on the initiative of Papen, to accept the appointment of Hitler as chancellor in the mistaken belief that Hitler could be 'tamed' to suit the interests of the conservative establishment.

The various attempts to restructure the state and to achieve an authoritarian solution to Germany's crisis in 1932-3 all came to nothing because of a lack of popular support. Germany was a modern society in an age of mass politics and it was no longer so easy to brush aside the wishes of the people. Nazi political strength was only too apparent in the election results, and their exclusion from the political process at a time of great socio-economic distress simply resulted in desperate violence in the streets between the various paramilitary groups, which in turn exacerbated the atmosphere of crisis. By January 1933 the clique of personalities around President Hindenburg was divided and no longer capable of governing the country on its own. In the end they had run out of political alternatives which excluded Hitler and the Nazis.

5 When and Why did Weimar Democracy Die?

It is now clear that when Hitler became chancellor on 30 January 1933 Weimar democracy was already dead. The problem for the historian is trying to determine when Weimar actually expired and why. In the view of the pessimists Weimar had been a 'gamble which stood virtually no chance of success' (Feldman); for the ultra-optimists there continued to be alternatives and the chance of democratic survival until mid-1932 when Papen became chancellor and the July elections resulted in such a dramatic polarisation (see the table on page 140). Caught between these two extremes the history student might feel lost - if the experts cannot agree, who am I to suggest an answer? Alternatively, and more cynically, he/she might assume that any old conclusion will do. Such views would be naive. Most historical writing is essentially a personal and provisional interpretation of the past and there are very few 'correct' answers. However, if it is to be good history, any interpretation must have examined the evidence and provided convincing explanations which are intellectually satisfying and coherent. Interpretations of Weimar's disintegration will therefore differ. Over the years historians with very different perspectives have emphasised different aspects or applied different criteria and, as we have seen, this is an on-going process. What follows is just one of many possible explanations. It should certainly not be regarded as a definitive answer to the above question.

From its inception the democratic republic was confronted by the hostility of Germany's established elites. In the wake of military defeat and the threat of revolution this opposition was at first constrained. However, the fact that so many key figures in German society and business rejected democracy and wished to dismantle the political and social compromise of 1918 in the hope of re-establishing the pre-war order represented a latent weakness. It acted as a powerful handicap to the successful evolution of the republic in the 1920s and in the 1930s it was to become a decisive factor in the final collapse of Weimar.

The republic was also dogged by almost continuous economic crisis whose effects permeated virtually all levels of society. It inherited the enormous costs and effects of the First World War and unfortunately for democracy's reputation and stability this burden persisted in various forms - post-war reconstruction, Allied reparations and the huge cost of pensions. So, even though the inflation crisis was surmounted, it is now appreciated that fundamental structural problems in the economy remained unresolved and they were to have dramatic consequences with the onset of the world economic crisis.

Weimar democracy never really enjoyed widespread political support, in the sense that there was never wholehearted acceptance of and confidence in the system and its values. From the republic's birth its relatively narrow base of popular support was caught between the extremes of left and right. As time progressed, Weimar's claims to legitimacy became ever more open to question. Democracy was associated - however unjustly - with defeat and the humiliation of Versailles and reparations. Its reputation was further impaired by the crisis of 1922-3. It is surely significant that by 1928 the cause of German middle-class liberalism, which should have been a mainstay of the republic, was in electoral decline and that the Centre and DNVP were both moving to the right. Even the loyalty and the commitment to democracy of the SPD, Weimar's largest party until 1932, have to be offset by the recognition that it was resented as a coalition partner and ostracised by its left-wing partner. In short, a significant proportion of the German population had little faith in the existing constitutional arrangements and was looking for change.

The force of these on-going pressures meant that Weimar democracy went through a number of phases. The difficult circumstances of its birth in 1918-19 left it handicapped and it was a major achievement in many respects that it successfully survived the problems of the period 1919 to 1923. However, the years of relative stability from 1923 to 1929 amounted to only a short respite and they did not result in a significant maturation or strengthening of the Weimar system. On the eve of the world economic crisis it seems that Weimar's long-term chances of survival were already less than good.

In the end, the impact of the world depression exacerbated the underlying pressures which then interacted to bring about Weimar's final crisis. The manner of Brüning's appointment and the resort to rule by emergency decree created *de facto* another system of government - the presidential regime. This was soon followed by the electoral breakthrough of the Nazis. From this time democracy's chance of recovering the political initiative was slim indeed - the only realistic options available all revolved around some variant of authoritarian rule. The spiritual flame of democracy may have continued to burn - albeit with ever decreasing brightness - until it was finally extinguished by the Nazis in early 1933, but democratic rule in Germany had actually died in the spring and summer of 1930.

Making notes on 'Weimar: the Final Years'

This is a vital chapter, but it cannot be understood in isolation. It really builds upon all your previous work on Weimar and of course, it is closely tied to your study of the rise of Nazism. Before making notes, study the summary diagram below very carefully to see how the disintegration of Weimar democracy resulted from a variety of pressures.

The level of detail required from your notes in this chapter needs to be thought about carefully. Your main objective is to understand the major historical forces at work and to put them into some kind of context in your own mind. But unless you also appreciate the role of the key personalities in the intrigue you will get confused. The following headings should help you:

1. The Impact of the Depression. List and explain all the major economic and social effects of the depression in Germany. Why was Germany so badly affected by the world depression?

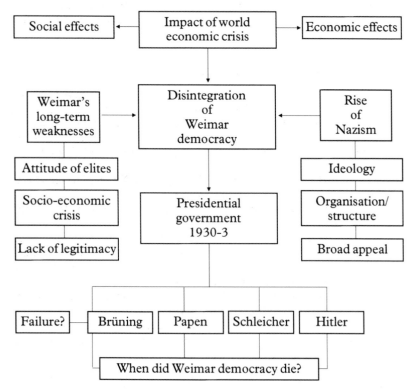

Summary - Weimar: the Final Years

2. Chancellor Brüning, 1930-2.
2.1 The advent of presidential government.
2.2 Coping with the Depression. Examine carefully the arguments of Borchardt and Holtfrerich.
2.3 Brüning's fall. What were the decisive factors in Brüning's fall from power?
2.4 Assessment. A failure? A tragic failure? A victim of circumstances? An incompetent? Look back at your notes for the last four sub-sections. Why do you think historians have devoted so much time to research and analysis of Brüning's chancellorship? Why is he still such a controversial figure?
3. The Rise of National Socialism. Study the table of Weimar election results on page 140. Write an analysis of the elections of 1930-2 explaining how and why the main parties gained or lost. Why did Nazism emerge as the main threat to the Weimar Republic?
4. The Final Months of the Republic. What were the aims of Papen, Schleicher and Hindenburg? Why did they fail to achieve a political solution without the involvement of the Nazis?
5. The Death of Weimar Democracy. Read section 5 very carefully and without reference to the text write a summary in no more than 100 words. Do you agree with the author's conclusion?

Answering essay questions on 'Weimar: the Final Years'

It is unlikely that you will be set essay questions which focus solely on material from this chapter. Questions on Weimar tend to be broad and will probably require a good general knowledge and understanding of the entire period. Some may even require reference back to Imperial Germany or, even more likely, an appreciation of the rise of Nazism.

1. To what extent is it right to state that the Weimar Republic was swept away in an economic blizzard?
2. Why was the Weimar Republic able to resist non-democratic forces in the 1920s, but not in the 1930s?
3. 'By the end of 1932 the collapse of the Weimar Republic had become inevitable: Hitler's accession to power had not'. Discuss.
4. Would you agree that the depression was not so much the cause as the occasion of Weimar's collapse?
5. 'A noble experiment with positive achievements'. Is this a fair judgement of the Weimar Republic?
6. What were the weaknesses of the Weimar Republic?
7. Why was 'the Weimar Republic opposed by every influential group in Germany'?

These questions vary quite considerably in their degree of difficulty. Try to think of the problems each one is likely to create, for example:

- the degree of detail/timing?
- organisation/structure/balance?
- definitions/concepts?
- assumptions?

Rearrange the questions in order of difficulty. Which one do you think is the easiest to tackle? Which one is the hardest?

You may feel that question 6 is relatively straightforward because it could be answered by merely describing a number of weaknesses. But presumably a lot of other students would think along these lines as well! How can you write an answer that would impress and gain high marks? One way is to think of and then discuss a number of sub-questions:
- Was Weimar decisively weakened by the circumstances of its birth?
- Were Weimar's weaknesses a result of external or internal pressures?
- How significantly did 1923 weaken Weimar?
- Why did Weimar's weaknesses only come to a head in the early 1930s?

In this way as long as you keep the key word 'weakness' in mind all the time you can write a much more profound essay.

On the other hand, although the assertion in Question 3 is quite clear, you may feel that the task of organising an answer is a daunting one. See if you can draw up a plan for this essay question, bearing in mind its implications: that Weimar's weaknesses (relative to its strengths) were so fundamental that its collapse was 'inevitable'; that Hitler's political position was not strong enough to guarantee his accession; that other political outcomes were a real possibility.

Question 7 is also awkward. Can you see what the problem is? If you can also develop an argument with evidence which throws doubt on the assumption of the question, then you will be well rewarded by the examiner.

Source-based questions on 'Weimar: the Final Years'

1 Brüning's Fall from Power
Read the extracts from General Groener and the Nazi propaganda chief Goebbels on pages 137 and 138. Answer the following questions.
a) Explain Goebbels's phrase 'Presidential Cabinet' (line 6).
   (2 marks)
b) Why was Goebbels so pleased about the outcome of Hitler's interview with the President? (4 marks)
c) What impression does Goebbels convey about the state of German politics in 1932? How reliable do you think were his impressions?
   (4 marks)
d) Groener was forced to resign his post a few days before Brüning. To what extent do you think this may have affected his assessment?
   (4 marks)
e) To what extent do these two sources agree upon the circumstances of Brüning's fall? (6 marks)

CHAPTER 8

Conclusion: Imperial and Weimar Germany in the Context of Modern German History

History is not a static discipline. It is an ongoing subject of study, which means that there is a continuous interplay of ideas at work. Interpretations are being constantly refined, opposed or revived and this may make the subject appear rather frustrating to the student at first. In fact, it is a reflection of the subject's vitality and the specific historical debates which have arisen from the study of imperial and Weimar Germany are a perfect example of this. However, periods of history must not be seen in isolation and over the years some of the most heated (and interesting) discussion has been generated by those historians who have attempted to explain modern German history in its broader context. These controversies have focussed on two main themes: the concept of a German *Sonderweg* or 'special path of development'; and the issue of continuity.

1 A German *Sonderweg?*

The idea of a German *Sonderweg* is far from new. It dates back to the nineteenth century and although it has been interpreted in very different ways, in essence it suggests that German history diverged from the history of other countries and as a result Germany's path to modernisation was somehow peculiar. In the years before 1945 the German *Sonderweg* was usually portrayed in a positive light. German academics, particularly during the Wilhelmine period, schooled in the conservative-nationalist tradition, tended to extol Germany's political, military and economic success as resulting from the values of discipline and order which permeated society and from the superior quality and efficiency of institutions, such as the civil service, the army and the education system. And this tendency was perpetuated in a kind of nostalgic after-glow as Germany experienced the various traumas of the period 1914 to 1945.

However, in the wake of the defeat and destruction of World War Two and the revelations about the true nature of the Nazi regime, the notion of a German *Sonderweg* underwent a dramatic reversal of interpretation. The desire to understand and explain the Third Reich led many historians, especially in the 1960s, to conclude that its origins were to be found in certain peculiar aspects of Germany's development in the nineteenth century. It was generally perceived that somewhere along the road to modernisation Germany had taken a wrong turning and as a result it had not evolved in the normal way. Exponents of this negative *Sonderweg* focused on various aspects of German history: some saw the Prussian army and its militarist ethos as the key; others examined Germany's intellectual history and claimed to identify a certain kind of 'German mind'. Most compelling of all though was the argument of those structuralist historians in Germany, epitomised by Wehler. They argued that the direction of German history until 1945 could essentially be explained by the contrast between Germany's economic growth and progress and the lack of development in the realm of political and social affairs. In their view, the failure of the German bourgeoisie to bring about a liberal revolution in 1848, followed by the imposed unification of Bismarck, allowed the power and status of the traditional elites to persist. As a result, industrialisation in Germany took place, unlike in Britain and the USA, within an authoritarian monarchical political system which maintained the political impotence of the middle classes and suppressed the working classes.

In Germany the use by structuralist historians of the German *Sonderweg* in a negative sense assumed the status of an established orthodoxy in the 1960s and 1970s. To some extent this was a natural outgrowth of Fischer's thesis (see page 41) which had unequivocally laid the blame on Germany for starting World War One. It also reflected the methodological shift initiated by Fischer's advocacy of the 'primacy of domestic politics'. However, perhaps most significantly, it underlined the changing perception of Germany's younger generation of historians towards their subject. There was a growing feeling that, in a democratic and pluralist society such as Germany had become, they had to promote its values and virtues. To this end they needed to educate the nation in the reality of its past and to reject any attempts to provide an apologia for Nazism. In the light of these honourable objectives it is perhaps not so surprising that the first doubts about the validity of a negative *Sonderweg* emanated not from within Germany but from outside.

In the 1980s the British historians Blackbourn and Eley prompted a minor furore in the German historical profession by questioning the validity of the *Sonderweg* concept as a tool for historical analysis. They argued that attempts to explain German history by reference to a wrong path had uncritically employed western countries, and especially Britain, as their benchmark for 'normality'. This approach had encouraged a tendency amongst such historians to look for 'the sins of omission of one national history when measured against other idealised national histories', which had resulted in an exaggeration of the 'peculiarity' of Germany's path to modernisation. In effect, the Blackbourn and Eley thesis represented a plea to break free from the constraints of the *Sonderweg* straitjacket, with its narrow focus on the all-pervasive domination of the conservative elites. They argued that there was a need to examine what 'actually did happen in German history' in its broadest sense, and then to compare Germany with a variety of European states, and not just with Britain.

The criticisms by Blackbourn and Eley of the negative *Sonderweg* were at first generally not well received by structuralist historians in Germany. However, in the longer term their effect has been to stimulate debate and to encourage new lines of research. There has been an extensive growth in *Alltagsgeschichte* (the history of everyday life) which has shifted the emphasis of historical research away from the political centre and towards both the grassroots of society and the different regions of Germany. This has had the effect of opening up new and diverse avenues in the explanation and interpretation of German history. However, detailed research into the comparative histories of Germany and other European states still remains limited, though early investigations suggest that there was no one clear path for societies undergoing modernisation. Indeed, it seems that the variety of developmental paths pursued by European states makes it difficult to correlate political and socio-economic development into any kind of 'normal' model. Some countries, such as France (the Second Empire) and Italy (Fascism), experienced authoritarian regimes during indus-trialisation, while others, such as Britain and Belgium, did not. On the other hand, non-industrialised states went their different ways as well: some, like those in Scandinavia, were still able to evolve into mature and sophisticated democracies, whereas others like Spain (under Franco) and Portugal (under Salazaar) became authoritarian dictatorships. If such comparisons are indeed valid, then perhaps historians must no longer assume that Germany's road to modernisation was any more 'special' or 'peculiar' than any other European state. In that way the concept of a German *Sonderweg* (whether positive or negative) may well be a thing of the past.

2 Continuity and Fluidity in Modern German History

Closely entwined with the *Sonderweg* debate is another central issue of German history: the extent to which one can identify within it continuity or continuities. Initially, after the demise of the Third Reich Germany's conservative-nationalist historians tended to view Hitler and Nazism in rather apologetic terms as an aberration totally at odds with Germany's historical development under the *Kaiserreich* and the Weimar Republic. For them 1933 marked a radical break. However, in the wake of the 'Fischer controversy' most historians have come to see continuity as an essential concept on which to build their interpretations of Germany, 1871-1945. Structuralists have focused on the continuity provided by the role of the elites and their methods of political manipulation. And even many revisionist opponents of structuralism generally endorse the existence of important strands of continuity. Röhl readily identifies the essential continuity provided by such themes as war aims and armaments policy. Blackbourn and Eley likewise do not deny the continuity, but prefer to shift the focus onto the theme of the popular social and political roots of National Socialism.

However, any move towards consensus over the significance of the continuity concept as a tool for understanding modern German history, should not lull the student into the trap of assuming that such continuities only allow German history, like Taylor's river (see page 2), to flow in one direction. It is all too easy perhaps to highlight those elements which help to explain later developments whilst playing down others which might imply another outcome. For this reason the continuities of German history must not be allowed to disguise the fact that the period 1890-1933 was in reality rather more fluid - or open-ended - than is often assumed.

Imperial Germany on the eve of the First World War was a land of contrasts - a complex mixture of forces for change and forces of conservatism. However, it was an essentially civilised nation. It enjoyed a highly sophisticated cultural tradition and an advanced education system. And, despite the authoritarian constitution, the values of the *Kaiserreich* were squarely in the tradition of what the Germans call the *Rechtsstaat* (the constitutional state). Citizens enjoyed certain legal rights which meant for example that only civilian courts could curtail an individual's liberty. Recent research into Wilhelmine social history also suggests that on balance Germany was not nearly so backward-looking in its social attitudes as has often been thought. It has been claimed that the officer corps of the army and, particularly, the navy were increasingly drawn from the middle classes; that wealthy industrialists did not as a rule feel the need to 'ape' the aristocracy in their life-style and took pride in their entrepreneurial achievements; and that even the *Junkers* were beginning to adapt their farming methods to the demands of a modern industrial economy. Finally, in the sphere of politics it should be remembered that although this period witnessed the emergence of radical nationalism and the mass membership of the various nationalistic interest groups such as the Navy League, the most popular party in the *Kaiserreich* was the SPD, which, despite its revolutionary rhetoric, had become increasingly reformist in practice. Its growing concern with living and working conditions, its desire to be 'legal' and finally, its infamous vote in favour of the war credits all help to suggest that the Social Democrats were no longer moving in the direction of socialist revolution, but rather towards some kind of political accommodation with the Wilhelmine state.

In the light of such developments, it would seem more accurate to conclude that in 1914 Germany could have evolved along any one of several different lines of historical development and that in the long-term, genuine parliamentary democracy was just as feasible as authoritarian dictatorship. However, this relatively open-ended situation was clearly upset by the onset of the First World War and, more particularly, by the traumatic impact of the later war years and the post-war crisis. 1917-20 were perhaps the most crucial years in the period 1890-1933, for they witnessed the vital developments which later made the Nazi dictatorship possible. Politically, the war resulted in the growth of a radicalised nationalism, fuelled by dreams of territorial expansion and increasingly prone to expressions of virulent racism. At the same time, the divisions within the socialist movement did little to calm the fears of its conservative and liberal opponents, which were actually increased by events in Russia. In the economic sphere the country lost vital markets and incurred massive debts which laid the basis for the subsequent inflation crisis. In addition, the effects of war upon society were to create considerable hardship and bitterness which exaggerated the tendency towards polarisation. All these factors contributed to the demise of the *Kaiserreich*, but the shock of defeat, the *Diktat* of Versailles and the ongoing socio-economic problems perpetuated the crisis beyond 1918 and weakened Weimar's claims to popular legitimacy from the start. On top of all this, Weimar's compromises with the traditional elites enabled the forces of conservatism to survive and to work for constitutional reaction from within.

Even so, such handicaps did not doom Weimar from the start. In many respects it was a major achievement and a sign of Weimar's inner strengths that it successfully survived the crisis year of 1923. However, the failure of parliamentary democracy to build on the relatively favourable circumstances of 1924-9 suggests that the odds on its survival were progressively lengthening. The onset of the world economic crisis witnessed the re-emergence with renewed vigour of the old continuities, partially dormant in the 1920s. From 1930 democracy was almost certain to give way to a brand of authoritarianism supported by the elites, which would vehemently oppose socialism and favour an expansionist foreign policy. This is not to say that it had to take the form of a Nazi dictatorship, but as the popular support for National Socialism grew, it became increasingly difficult to ignore its claim to participate in government.

Continuity in history must never be confused with inevitability. There were powerful and crucial continuities which helped to shape the history of Germany from 1890 to 1933. However, these continuities and the added advantage of hindsight should not lull the historian into a false determinism. Imperial and Weimar Germany was a society undergoing the transitional problems of modernisation and as a result there was a host of political, economic, social and cultural forces at work. This suggests that Germany could have evolved along any one of several alternate paths, though the available options were progressively reduced as time passed by. In that sense Germany's historical development, although deeply influenced by its continuities, was actually more fluid than is often supposed.

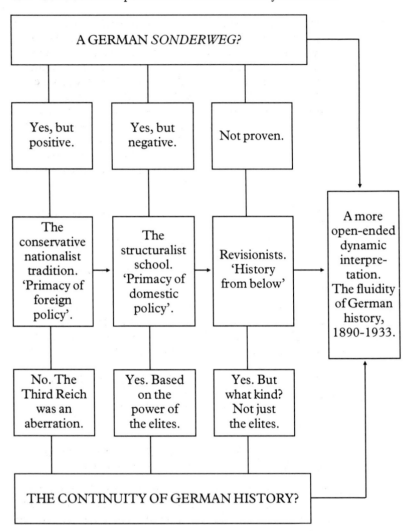

Summary - Conclusion: Imperial and Weimar Germany in Context

Working on *'Conclusion: Imperial and Weimar Germany in the Context of Modern German History'*

You are unlikely to be set essay questions which require a general analysis of the entire period 1890-1933, let alone 1871-1945. However, your time will not be wasted, if you apply yourself to this last chapter, because it should enable you to start putting imperial and Weimar Germany into a broader historical context. This may seem rather vague and perhaps unappealing at first, but if it is done well, it will pay rich dividends. Essays from students who have got beneath the surface of a topic, inevitably stand out simply because they so obviously exhibit a greater intellectual depth and more sophisticated patterns of thought. There are two strategies open to you, then. If you feel that you are not yet ready to confront the broad issues, simply re-read the chapter, study the summary diagram and make a brief one-sentence written note on each paragraph. Perhaps it would be a good idea to come back to this chapter after you have finished your study of the Third Reich. If you want to take the chapter further, you should do the following. Re-read the whole chapter slowly and then study the summary diagram very carefully. Now try to explain in your own words:

a) how each school of historians stands on the issue of the 'German *Sonderweg*';
b) how each school of historians stands on the issue of 'Continuity in German History';
c) why the idea of a more fluid/open-ended interpretation of modern German history has evolved.

This should provide you with a framework of ideas, but now you have got to start to decide where you stand on these issues by thinking them through. A good way to achieve this is to examine some of the more extreme points of view. Study the following statements:

a) 'The crucial continuity in German history from 1871-1945 was the dominating influence of the Prussian elites.'
b) 'The idea of a German *Sonderweg* is a myth.'
c) '1933 was the key turning-point in German history in the period 1871-1945.'
d) 'Without the First World War Wilhemine Germany would have evolved into a well-established constitutional monarchy.'

For each statement write about 100 words in support of the assertion and then about 100 words to oppose it. Finally, write a concluding assessment, which tries to make an overall judgement about the quotation. For example:

i) totally agree or disagree, but say why you are so certain;
ii) essentially agree or disagree, but recognise that it is important not to forget the significance of other factor(s);
iii) cannot decide - the evidence is not clear-cut and a reasoned 'don't know' is required.

Chronological Table

1871		Proclamation of German Empire and creation of Bismarckian constitution.
1879		Introduction of agricultural and industrial tariffs.
1888	15 June	Accession of Wilhelm II.
1890	18 March	Dismissal of Bismarck. Appointment of Caprivi.
	Oct.	Anti-socialist laws came to an end.
1891		Reform of Tariff Act (1879). Led to bi-lateral commercial treaties, 1891-4.
		Caprivi's social reforms introduced.
1894		Dual Alliance signed between France and Russia.
		Proposal by Kaiser of Anti-Socialist Subversion Bill came to nothing.
		Resignation of Caprivi. Appointment of Hohenlohe.
1897		Reorganisation of government. Bülow appointed foreign minister.
		Advent of *Weltpolitik*.
1898	April	First Navy Law passed by *Reichstag*.
1898-1901		Failure of Anglo-German alliance negotiations.
1900	June	Second Navy Law passed by *Reichstag*.
	Oct.	Bülow appointed chancellor.
1902	Dec.	Tariff Law passed. Agricultural tariffs raised.
1904	April	Entente Cordiale between Britain and France.
1904-5		Hottentot revolt in German SW Africa.
1905		Collapse of Bülow's budget proposals.
1905-6		First Moroccan Crisis.
1906		Supplementary Navy Law.
1907	Jan.	Hottentot election. Creation of Bülow bloc.
	Aug.	Anglo-Russian entente.
1908		Eulenburg homosexuality scandal.
		Daily Telegraph affair.
1909	March	Rejection of Bülow's budget by *Reichstag*.
	July	Resignation of Bülow. Appointment of Bethmann-Hollweg as chancellor.
1911		Seconnd Moroccan Crisis.
1912	Jan.	*Reichstag* election. SPD became largest party.
	Dec.	War Council meeting.
1913		Army Bill increased peace-time strength of army by 20 per cent. Financed by introduction of property tax.
	Oct.	Zabern affair.
1914	28 June	Assassination of Franz Ferdinand in Sarajevo.
	23 July	Austro-Hungarian ultimatum to Serbia.
	31 July	Russian mobilization.
	1 Aug.	German declaration of war on Russia.

	3 Aug.	German declaration of war on France.
	4 Aug.	British declaration of war on Germany following German invasion of Belgium.
	Sept.	First battle of Marne.
1915	Feb.	Unrestricted submarine warfare introduced, but suspended after sinking of *Lusitania*.
1916	Feb.	Unrestricted submarine warfare briefly reintroduced.
	April	Resignation of Tirpitz. Battles of Verdun and, from July, Battle of Somme.
	Aug.	Establishment of 'silent dictatorship' under Hindenburg and Ludendorff.
	Dec.	Introduction of Auxiliary Service Law.
1917	Feb.	Unrestricted submarine warfare reintroduced for duration of war.
	April	Declaration of war by USA on Germany. Split in SPD.
	July	Peace Resolution passed by *Reichstag*. Resignation of Bethmann.
1918	March	Treaty of Brest-Litovsk. Launch of German offensive in the west.
	8 August	'Black day' for the German army on western front.
	Sept.	Collapse of Germany's allies.
	Oct.	Appointment of Prince Max von Baden as chancellor and the introduction of constitutional reforms.
	3 Nov.	Sailors' revolt at Kiel.
	9 Nov.	Abdication of Kaiser. Declaration of republic. Formation of provisional government coalition under Ebert.
	10 Nov.	Ebert-Groener pact.
	11 Nov.	Armistice signed.
	15 Nov.	Stinnes-Legien agreement.
1919	Jan.	Spartakist uprising defeated by *Freikorps*.
	19 Jan.	Election of first National Assembly.
	April	Short-lived Soviet Republic in Bavaria.
	28 June	Treaty of Versailles signed.
	31 July	Adoption of Weimar constitution.
1920	March	Kapp putsch.
1921	March	Armed uprising by communists in Saxony.
	May	IARC announced reparations bill of £6,600m.
1922	April	Failure of Genoa Economic Conference. Treaty of Rapallo between Germany and USSR.
	June	Assassination of Rathenau.
1923	Jan.	Occupation of Ruhr by France and Belgium commenced.
	Aug.	Stresemann appointed chancellor: 'passive resistance' ended; *Rentenmark* introduced.

	8 Nov.	Nazi Beer Hall *putsch* in Munich: disastrous fiasco.
1924		Introduction of state arbitration scheme to settle industrial disputes.
	Aug.	Dawes Plan accepted by Germany.
1925	Feb	Death of Ebert. Election of Field Marshall Hindenburg as president.
	Oct.	Locarno treaties signed.
1926	April	Treaty of Berlin between Germany and USSR.
	Sept.	Germany joined League of Nations.
1928		Germany signed Kellogg-Briand Pact.
	May	*Reichstag* election. Formation of Müller government.
1929	Aug.	Young Plan agreed.
	Oct.	Death of Gustav Stresemann. Wall Street Crash.
	Dec.	National referendum on Young Plan.
1930	Mar.	Collapse of Müller's coalition government. Appointment of Brüning as chancellor.
	Sept.	*Reichstag* election: Nazis emerged as second largest party.
1932	Apr.	Re-election of Hindenburg as president.
	June	Abolition of reparations payments at Lausanne conference.
	May	Forced resignation of Brüning. Papen became chancellor.
	July	*Reichstag* election: Nazis by far the largest party
	Nov.	*Reichstag* election.
	Dec.	Resignation of Papen. Appointment of Schleicher as chancellor
1933	Jan.	Germany's unemployment reached 6.1 millions.
	30 Jan.	Hitler appointed Chancellor.

Glossary

ADV
: *Alldeutsche Verband.* Pan-German League. Right-wing nationalist interest group.

Anschluss
: Union. Unification of Germany and Austria.

Beamte
: State official.

BdL
: *Bund der Landwirte.* Farmers' League. Lobby for high tariffs.

Burgfriede
: Political truce.

Diktat
: Right-wing description of Versailles treaty. Literally, a 'dictated' peace.

Ersatzkaiser
: Literally 'substitute kaiser'. A reference given to the powers endowed upon the Weimar presidency.

Flottenverein
: Navy League. Nationalist interest group set up to press for increased naval spending.

Führerprinzip
: The leadership principle.

Gau
: Region. Basic unit of Nazi organization.

Junker
: Prussian landowner.

Kaiserreich
: Imperial Germany 1871-1918.

KRA
: *Kriegsrohstoffabteilung.* War raw materials department.

Kulturkampf
: Cultural struggle. Bismarck's anti-Catholic policy of the 1870s.

Landtag
: Provincial parliament.

Lebensraum
: Living-space. Policy of expansion into eastern Europe.

Mittelstand
: Middle class. Traditionally referred to the artisan/shopkeeper rather than the new industrialists.

OHL
: *Oberste Heeresleitung.* Supreme Army Command.

Rechtsstaat
: Constitutional state based upon the rule of law.

Reichsrat
: Second chamber of German parliament, representing federal provinces.

Rentenmark
: New currency introduced in 1924.

Sammlungspolitik
: Literally a 'policy of concentration'. Term used by structuralists to describe the attempt by the elites to rally the middle and upper classes behind the imperial regime.

Sonderweg
: Special path. Used in various senses to suggest that German history was different to the norm.

Spartakusbund
: Spartakist League. Group of extreme left-wing socialists. Forerunner of Communist Party.

Weltpolitik
: Literally 'world policy'. Initiative launched by German government in 1897.

Further Reading

1. Textbooks

Because of the importance of Germany in modern European history there are a number of suitable general textbooks in print. By far the most thorough and readable survey is:
William Carr, *A History of Germany 1815-1990* (Edward Arnold, 4th ed. 1992).
More intellectually demanding are
Volker Berghahn, *Modern Germany* (CUP, 2nd ed. 1987), and
Gordon Craig, *Germany 1866-1945* (OUP 1981).

The emphasis and approach of these three books varies quite considerably. It would be a good idea to see if you can detect these differences by dipping into one or two of the relevant chapters of each book. You should not take detailed notes from them, but you could briefly note the 'line' taken by each author on the major issues.

2. Biographies

Because of the influence of the 'structuralist' school and its dislike of 'personalising' history, German academic historians have tended to fight shy of the biographical approach. Not even one full-scale biography of Wilhelm II has ever been written by a German university historian! The same can also be said of Brüning and Hindenburg! Stresemann and Ebert have not been so completely ignored, but none of the works have been translated.

However, if you would like to gain a feel for some of the personalities refer to:
J.C.G. Röhl, *The Kaiser and his Court* (Cambridge 1994). This is a stimulating and scholarly work based on an exhaustive analysis of original sources. Particularly recommended are chapters 1, 4 & 7.
J. Wright, 'Stresemann and Weimar' in *History Today*, October 1989. A brief, but excellent article which reassesses his career.

3. Specialist Studies

If you wish to study some of the historical controversies more deeply you will need to select your reading with great care. The academic literature on German history is immense and much of it is detailed and very specialised. The following are suggested 'starting-points':
H-U. Wehler, *The German Empire* (Leamington Spa 1984). This is a difficult read, even in translation! Have a look at pp.52-99 and 192-246.
V. Berghahn, *Germany and the Approach of War in 1914* (London 1973).

R. Evans, 'Kaiser Wilhelm and German History' in *History Review* Issues 10 & 11 in 1991. A good review of the main themes.

F. Fischer, *From Kaiserreich to Third Reich* (Unwin & Hyman 1986). The best brief introduction to Fischer's thinking (99 pages!).

E. Kolb, *The Weimar Republic* (Unwin & Hyman 1988). A thorough and clearly written historical and historiographical survey.

D. Peukert, *The Weimar Republic* (Penguin 1991). An original and thought-provoking approach.

A. de Jonge, *The Weimar Chronicle*. Not really a history book, but an attempt to capture the mood of Weimar Germany.

I. Kershaw (ed), *Weimar; Why did German Democracy Fail* (Weidenfeld & Nicholson 1990). Mainly concentrates on the economic aspects of the debate.

A.J. Nicholls, *Weimar and the Rise of Hitler* (Macmillan, 3rd ed. 1991).

4. Sources

There is no definitive collection of documents in English covering the whole period 1890-1933, but a good range of material is provided by:

J. Laver (ed.), *Imperial and Weimar Germany 1890-1933* (Hodder & Stoughton 1992).

J.C.G. Röhl, *From Bismarck to Hitler* (Longmans 1970).

For a full range of statistical data turn to:

V. Berghahn, see above, pp.269-312. 55 tables on politics, economics and social trends.

Acknowledgements

The publishers would like to thank the following for permission to reproduce material in this volume:

Cambridge University Press for extracts from *Kaiser Wilhelm II: New Interpretations*, Röhl, (1982) and *Modern Germany,* Bergahn, (1987); Longman Group Ltd for extracts from *Weimar Republic,* Hiden, (1974) and *From Bismarck to Hitler,* Röhl, (1970); Ewan MacNaughton Associates on behalf of *The Telegraph* Plc for an article from *The Daily Telegraph,* (1908); Oswald Wolff Publishers Ltd for extracts from *Upheaval and Continuity,* ed. E. J. Feuchtwanger (taken from the chapter *The Weimar Republic - Failure and Prospects of German Democracy* by Kurt Sontheimer), (1973); Poem by Bruno Frank *(Proud Times)* and Meinke letter quoted in *Germany 1866-1945,* by Gordon A. Craig, (1978) by permission of the Oxford University Press; Allen Lane the Penguin Press for data of prices quoted in *The Weimar Republic,* by Detleve J.K. Peukert, trans. by Richard Devson, (1991); Jonathan Cape for extracts from *Dreadnought,* by Robert K. Massie, (1991); Weidenfeld and Nicolson for extracts from *Weimar: Why did German Democracy Fail?* ed. Kershaw, (1990) Dr Alan White for his translation of *Vowärts* obituary, p. 125. Every effort has been made to trace and acknowledge ownership of copyright. The publishers will be glad to make suitable arrangements with any copyright holders whom it has not been possible to contact.

Index